the velveteen mommy

For Ben,
who always laughs at my jokes, never at my dreams

In memory of
Helen Amelia Baldwin
(May 1, 1939–August 18, 1989),
a true Velveteen Mommy

contents

acknowledgments

a t the outset of my career, I, along with a group of other aspiring writers, conceived and gave birth to a fledgling writers' group. For lack of a better name, we first called it the Snohomish Writers' Group. It has since been named SWiG, in honor of our tradition of toasting each other's publishing triumphs with sparkling cider in Dixie cups. To a large degree, this book exists in its current stage because of that group's editorial labor of love. Special thanks to: Kari Brodin, Laura Christianson, Robin Chukitus, Janet McElvane, Sheri Plucker, and Cindy Rodland. Starbucks is on me next time, girlfriends!

My agent, Chip MacGregor, is a friend first and foremost. It has been such a blessing to have his friendship and now professional representation. Tally ho, my good man!

Rachelle Gardner, my editor at NavPress, has become an invaluable source of literary advice. I thank her for sharing my vision and taking a risk with an unknown writer. You're the best, Rachelle! Nicci Jordan, also at NavPress, has been my go-to girl for all my newbie questions. Thanks for hanging in there with me, Nicci!

I want to thank J.J., Katie, and Emma for providing daily material and for sharing in the excitement of writing my first book.

In more than one way, this book would not exist without them.

I would be remiss if I didn't mention the amazing Egge family and my gratitude to them for their support. I hold them accountable for passing on their quirky Norwegian sense of humor. Thanks to Dad, Mom, Tif, and Kim.

Ben, my sweet husband of thirteen years, has been an unwavering source of encouragement for me. He's my official rah-rah guy. To borrow the words from Philippians 1:3, I thank my God every time I remember him. Thanks for believing in me and for being such a good sport, Douce. I love you.

More than anything, I want to offer this book as a sacrifice of praise to my Lord and Savior, Jesus Christ. From the remnants of mistakes, frustrations, and toddler-trench moments, He has shaped and molded this manuscript in its entirety. And for some reason, He let me help! I thank you, Jesus, for being the Joy of my life.

BeCOMINg ReaL

*There is no escape when our Lord speaks. He always comes with
an arrestment of the understanding. Has the voice of God come to
you directly? If it has, you cannot mistake the intimate insistence
with which it has spoken to you in the language you know best,
not through your ears, but through your circumstances.*

OSWALD CHAMBERS

m y all-time favorite classic movie is *Please Don't Eat the
Daisies*, starring Doris Day and David Niven. In fact,
it's become my laundry-folding movie of choice. I think its appeal
stems from the hilarious scenes between Doris Day's character and
her four young sons. For some reason, the human spirit loves to
recognize that others have suffered (even in the make-believe world
of Hollywood) through the same painfully familiar experiences.

As each scene unfolds (sorry, I can't help the laundry
references), I mentally check off those situations to which my own
children have repeatedly exposed me. The kids run through the
house (check); they jump on the bed (check); they throw things out
their window (check); they eat in bed at night and make a mess of

their sheets (check); they gape at their mother as she dresses for a party, while commenting on her beautifying paraphernalia (check, check). While at school, one of the boys actually wedges his head in a chair and gets it stuck, to the dismay and frustration of his mother. A much-beloved scene for me is when one kiddo eats an arrangement of daisies because, as he puts it, "You didn't tell me not to!"

In our household, we've had so many "daisy-eating" types of episodes that the phone number for Poison Control has always been strategically displayed. In fact, for many years we had it memorized. Our babysitters get a little wide-eyed when we highlight that particular phone number before we escape for the evening. Indeed, we've called the number for Poison Control so many times that I once asked if they could ever use our file against us with Child Protective Services. (Little-known fact: All Poison Control files are confidential, so fear not, moms and dads.) I'm sure there has been or will be a time in your life when your offspring will attempt the unbelievable simply because you didn't tell them not to.

Sometimes those "you didn't tell me not to" moments add up to one exhausted mom. Over time, the tension builds and the inevitable Mommy Mania starts to rear its ugly head. When it happens to me, I tramp through the house muttering under my breath to no one in particular, "Am I the only one in the entire house who knows where the Legos go?" So I enjoy the smallest excuse to get away from my duties, even for an hour. My husband and I call it running away from home to find our marbles. Right about the time I threaten to superglue my kids' shoes to their perpetually bare feet, I get booted out of the house to find my marbles. Some of my favorite places for marble recovery are a coffee shop, a girlfriend's house, my favorite used bookstore, and women's church retreats. Upon reentering my

role as the nurturing caregiver of our home, my husband asks, "Did you talk a lot?" (There's really no question here—he's just humoring me), "Did you cry a lot?" and finally, "Did you laugh a lot?" God has created us to be women of emotions, hasn't He?

Those little escapes are necessary for my sanity. Sometimes I even daydream about what it would be like to live a life of leisure all the time: meeting girlfriends for coffee whenever I want, having time to read a book cover to cover, or even seeing a full-length feature film. But as appealing as that sounds, in my heart I know something would be missing. I might enjoy having all that time to myself, but then I wouldn't have the joys and the lessons my children bring every day. I would rather be like the Velveteen Rabbit— worn-out but well loved. How well I remember that story:

> There once was a velveteen rabbit, and in the beginning
> he was really splendid. He was fat [What?] and bunchy, as
> a rabbit should be; his coat was spotted brown and white,
> he had real thread whiskers, and his ears were lined with
> pink sateen. On Christmas morning, when he sat wedged
> in the top of the Boy's stocking, with a sprig of holly
> between his paws, the effect was charming.[1]

Can you recall what you were like before you had children? Unencumbered? Unfettered? Uninterrupted? Thinner? I can relate to the Velveteen Rabbit with sateen-lined ears. Perched upon my hospital bed the day our son was born, painkillers racing through my system, I felt quite splendid and charming. But the freshness of motherhood rubbed off, much like the newness of the Velveteen Rabbit.

Once the rabbit moved into the nursery, the boy forgot all about him and rather took him for granted. As time went on, the rabbit became the object of mockery by the other toys, which were much newer and more attractive than he.

Our culture sometimes doesn't look kindly upon the profession of motherhood. We are taken for granted, and sometimes even mocked. Success in our society is measured by take-home pay and bottom lines, not volunteer pay and clean bottoms. Too often, parental sacrifice is viewed as a futile exercise of misplaced talent. More than once, I have found myself steeped in the mire of what-ifs when I compare myself to others.

The only one who befriended the rabbit was the old skin horse, who was much older and wiser than all the other toys in the nursery. How grateful I am for my own "skin horses," those dear friends who have weathered through decades of motherhood and have helped me see beyond worldly entrapments.

> The Skin Horse had lived longer in the nursery than any of the others. He was so old that his brown coat was bald in patches and showed the seams underneath, and most of the hairs in his tail had been pulled out to string bead necklaces. He was wise, for he had seen a long succession of mechanical toys arrive to boast and swagger, and by-and-by break their mainsprings and pass away, and he knew that they were only toys, and would never turn into anything else.[2]

I have always loved this tender tale about the joys of loving and being loved, and of the pain of becoming Real. But I must admit, in

my younger days, I didn't get what it meant to become Real and why it would hurt. Once I began my journey of becoming a Real mom, I began to relate all-too-well to the "pain" part of the story:

> "What is REAL?" asked the Rabbit. . . .
>
> "Real isn't how you are made," said the Skin Horse. . . . When a child loves you for a long, long time, not just to play with, but REALLY loves you, then you become Real."
>
> "Does it hurt?" asked the Rabbit.
>
> "Sometimes," said the Skin Horse, for he was always truthful. "When you are Real you don't mind being hurt. . . . By the time you are Real, most of your hair has been loved off, and your eyes drop out and you get loose in the joints and all very shabby. But these things don't matter at all, because once you are Real you can't be ugly, except to people who don't understand."[3]

Oh, how ugly I feel sometimes! Not only are my joints looser and my hair rubbed off, but my bladder control has lost some of its pizzazz as well. Finding a stray gray hair, I am sorry to say, doesn't have the impact it once did; it has become an all-too-familiar experience for me. And while I'm feeling vulnerable, I'll briefly admit to the existence of a few age spots. Horrors!

In an astounding twist of Providence, God uses the true pain of motherhood to shape us, mold us, grow us, transform us, and make us Real—more like Himself: "Therefore we do not lose heart. Though outwardly we are wasting away, yet inwardly we are being renewed day by day" (2 Corinthians 4:16).

I think the Skin Horse was right: Becoming Real does hurt. But

it's not the nursery fairy that will render us Real at the end — it's Jesus, the One who loves us throughout the pain of motherhood as well as the pain of life.

My prayer is that you will find a miracle moment in your day — one of those ever-looked-for, never-really-expected gaps of time where you can escape to find your marbles while fingering through the pages of this book. My hope is that amidst the daily ups and downs of motherhood, when your hair is being rubbed off and you're feeling like a slightly shabby rendition of your former self, you will realize that a child loves you, and that means you're Real — a Real Velveteen Mommy.

taLes fRom tHe CRIB

> O sleep! O gentle sleep!
> Nature's soft nurse, how have I frighted thee,
> That thou no more wilt weigh my eyelids down,
> And steep my senses in forgetfulness?
>
> WILLIAM SHAKESPEARE

> People who say they sleep like a baby usually don't have one.
>
> LEO J. BURKE

I remember the exact moment I became a mother (it followed the pushing stage and preceded the stitches). It was only eight years ago, yet it seems like a lifetime. I was shocked at how difficult it was right from the get-go. Within moments of the umbilical cord being cut, I was thrust mercilessly into the bizarre world of parenting, starting with the mind-blowing experience of nursing.

How this one small (and apparently natural) act can cause so much stress and confusion for a room full of adults still baffles me. I remember strangers (okay, they were nurses) grabbing on to one

of my breasts and cramming it unceremoniously into my baby's mouth. Once we had attained the "latch," I was ordered to "maintain position" for thirty minutes, followed by thirty minutes on the other breast. This didn't seem so bad until the distressing reality of this scenario became apparent to me: The whole nursing procedure must be repeated every two hours, twenty-four hours a day, seven days a week until the baby is in college, or until you go crazy, whichever comes first. We won't even talk about nipple soreness or breast infections. This is supposed to be a family-friendly book.

Reflecting on the variety of discomforts present during the early baby stages, I have come to believe that somewhere in the world there is a government secretly using newborn infants to torture their political prisoners. And if there isn't, there should be. Think about it: getting ripped from sleep every two hours in order to drag yourself to the nearest chair to sit on a sore bottom while being handed a screaming baby who ravenously clamps onto you for a good sixty minutes. A lot of world problems could be resolved by using Operation Newborn.

Back before my life was blessed with babies, I was an *ER* junkie. We all know that *ER* is a modern version of a soap opera dressed up with chic actors and fewer cases of amnesia. One episode in particular stands out in my mind. Poor Chloe, Susan's drug-addicted homeless sister, had finally given birth to her illegitimate, Fetal Alcohol Syndrome baby, complete with the usual screaming and sweating Hollywood feels is necessary to include in a delivery scene. (Okay, what is with the sweating thing? I was dry as a bone all three times. Don't they realize that hospitals in real life have air conditioning going at full blast?) As the nurses thrust the squalling infant to Chloe's breast, she shrieked, "Ack! She feels like a human staple

gun!" To this day, that's the most honest description of the first-time nursing experience I've heard.

Besides the joys of nursing, the most surprising aspect of parenting is the whole sleeping thing—or total lack thereof. Before my first child was born, I dutifully attended a plethora of parenting and nursing classes provided by the hospital. I remember keeping notes on all the advice about necessary calories, newborn constipation, and nighttime colic. Surprisingly enough, none of these trained, trusted medical staff came close to mentioning the following terms: *staggering sleepiness, extreme exhaustion, flabbergasting fatigue,* and *plain old pooped!*

When my husband and I were newlyweds, several of our friends were in the early stages of parenthood. Somewhat envious of their growing families, I didn't pay much attention to the coincidental arrival of black circles under their eyes. Yearning for sympathy, they would moan about the exhaustion of parenting. I would roll my eyes and think rather self-righteously, *Good grief—get a grip! Take a nap! Have a cup of coffee. How hard can one baby be?* Boy, did I have a lot to learn. I think it's humorous in a sick sort of way that my second child didn't sleep through the night until she was three and a half years old.

Of course, I adore my children. And I really did love the baby stage. I even enjoyed nursing—after the first month, mind you. What I wasn't prepared for were the not-so-glorious moments in which my television-inspired fantasies about having a baby came crashing down on the rocks of reality. I had pictured my husband and me dressed like Paul and Jamie on *Mad About You*, in cool Gap outfits, continuing to live our lives (basically unchanged) as the baby slept quietly in the bassinet. We'd be bantering sitcom-like

humor as we encountered pithy issues such as "cloth or disposable" and "breast versus bottle."

Uh . . . *not*. Clearly, Paul and Jamie never experienced the joys of a real-live newborn. New mom Jamie appeared well rested, appropriately dressed, and lacking any visible evidence of baby spit-up or leaking milk on her clothes. She was even wearing makeup! Television simply does not do justice to the subject of becoming a parent. Did you ever see Jamie stand at the changing table going through two dozen baby wipes trying to clean the baby up after a particularly poopy diaper, only to finally give up and dunk the baby in the tub?

The whole diaper-changing thing is vastly misrepresented in the media. In fact, diaper commercial producers have a lot of explaining to do, in my opinion. No baby I've ever known has enjoyed having his or her diaper changed (and I used the expensive ones the first time). The nauseatingly cheerful diaper changer (actor) with the grin on his face is hilarious, if not absurd. Here's my diaper-changing credo: If, I repeat *if*, you're lucky enough to have a man in your life who will change a diaper, don't burden him with the expectation that he will enjoy it. It's a nasty task no matter how well the diaper is made, and don't let anybody tell you otherwise.

aDvIce aND coNseNt

I have always found it interesting how the opinions come out of the woodwork when you enter the world of parenthood. It starts with the names. Talk about pressure. When J.J. was six months old, we prepared to announce to my in-laws that we were expecting baby number two. We were more than a little nervous about how they

would take the news about us having another baby so soon—after all, we were still getting over the shock ourselves. Our fears turned out to be unfounded, and everything went fine. And then The Question came: "What are the names you've picked out?"

We collectively gulped and answered, "If it's a girl we're going to name her Katie Lynn, and if it's a boy he will be Samuel James." My husband's sweet grandma answered without missing a beat, "Well, you have plenty of time to change your mind!"

Then there's the ponderously prevalent problem of poundage. We get fat, and for some reason, other people notice. Non-pregnant people are obsessed with analyzing pregnant people's weight. I think a neon sign magically appears over a pregnant woman's head the day she conceives. This sign is invisible to the pregnant woman (and her husband, if he's smart); however, as it pulsates and hovers over her burgeoning body, its flashy message clearly reads to others: "So, what do you think of my pregnancy weight gain? Please, tell me what you think about it right now. After you are done with your scrutiny, make sure to put your hand right on my abdomen. Do not worry if you are a man and a complete stranger. I'm pregnant, so it's okay." (Did I mention that it's a really big sign?)

tHe LeaRNING cuRve

I'm a reader. I truly enjoy reading. I mean, it's sort of an obsession for me—possibly even an addiction. So, following my initiation to prenatal care, it made sense to accumulate and pore over a variety of books on the subjects of mothering, diapering, baby naming, teenage discipline, rocket science—you know, all the stuff a new parent needs to learn. I wanted the security of knowing I was going

to be prepared for *anything* that came along. I can already picture you smiling to yourself if you've spent any time with children. While books are excellent tools of the parenting trade, exasperation and experience has taught me far more. There is simply no way to prepare for everything that comes along with the role of maternity.

Some of the curves pitched over my home plate have sent me ducking for cover more than once. In fact, I started writing down the most helpful information I gleaned during pregnancy or shortly thereafter.

tHe top teN tHiNGs i LeaRNeD aBout HaviNG a BaBy

1. How to refer to my pregnancy progression in weeks, not months. To be truly hip in the pregnancy world, one must make this adaptation. Feel free to turn your nose up at the metric system; however, using the phrase, "I am seven months pregnant," is simply unacceptable in modern maternity circles.

2. The definitions of *episiotomy* and *epidural*. I remember feeling somewhat lost when these specific subjects came up in conversation. The first one always sounded like some type of surgery to remove an essential part of the brain, and I thought an epidural could possibly be some kind of thyroid medication. For your continuing education and information: An *episiotomy* (I am sorry to report) is "an incision into the perineum . . . to enlarge the space at the outlet."[4] You're going to have to look up the definition of perineum on your own; I'm not going there. An *epidural* is a procedure in which a nurse inserts a large needle into your back that somehow causes most of the childbirth

pain to disappear. I never have actually experienced an epidural. The only thing that disappeared for me was my pre-baby modesty.

3. The prudence of the phrase, "Never wake a sleeping baby."
4. Maternity clothes are only fun during your first pregnancy, and only *before* you begin to show. It basically goes downhill from there.
5. The existence of a product called nursing pads. I had never even heard of those before, nor did I realize how handy they are when you're in need of a coaster.
6. How the touch of a newborn can wondrously turn a grumpy old lady in the grocery store into an affectionate, nostalgic grandma. (Conversely, the sight of a newborn *with bare feet* can turn that nice older lady into a finger-wagging, head-shaking, disapproving lecturer.)
7. That JCPenney sends out an average of three photo coupons per week.
8. How much worse our labor is from everyone else's.
9. How much it hurts to have an earring ripped out by little fingers. I've given birth three times without drugs. I would prefer that over the pain of having my earlobes ripped in half by a feisty seven-month-old.
10. (This one's the kicker) How difficult it is to be truly selfless.

it's not all about me

There are a variety of benefits to having a baby besides the obvious blessing of snuggling with our precious progeny. Unfortunately, many of these benefits can also be accurately categorized as "lessons." For

me, new parenthood was a rude awakening to my own tendency toward self-absorption.

My first birthday after I was married (yet still childless) stands out as a stark illustration of my own selfishness. My dear husband presented me with roses, an evening out to dinner, and tickets to a chick flick. My response (I am loath to admit) was to spend the entire night pouting because it wasn't special enough. I was so young, and naive, and spoiled, and, well, self-centered. Ah, but becoming a mother changes all that, doesn't it? We don't have time to be selfish (not as much time anyway). These days, I am so thankful for time alone with my husband, and if food is involved, then it's a bonus. There were a few years in our married life with children when Communion at church constituted a date for us, and I was grateful for it, thank you very much.

If we're honest with ourselves, we realize the fact that we all struggle to differing degrees with self and selfishness. Being altruistic is not our natural tendency. The nature of motherhood forces us to put others and their needs first. I'm not going to try to tell you this is easy; you know better than that. Nevertheless, some of the most difficult things in life can bring us closer to God and teach us valuable lessons that stick with us the longest.

Many trials of new motherhood are momentary, and from a distance, most can be seen as humorous. However, parenthood does bring unique fiery trials in a variety of packages: watching a child face debilitating illness; struggling with a strong-willed and defiant child; experiencing relational issues with your children. The Pandora's Box of potential pain and difficulties we open when we become parents is immense, and thankfully only God can see into that future. The spiritual lessons we learn when we first become

parents are the jewels in the rough, blessings that come from learning the hard way to be selfless (is there an easy way?).

come to the cradle

Songwriter and singer Michael Card penned a lullaby several years ago titled "Come to the Cradle." In his book of the same name, Michael conveys the heart of the message of this song:

> The cradle calls us to come away from the busyness of the world—to rediscover the holy, unhurried life of a child, and to discover that as we pour ourselves into the lives of our little ones, life overflows in return. For the cry of a baby in the middle of the night is not simply a summons to change a diaper—it contains within it more than our ears can hear. It is a call to leave the cozy self-interest of our warm beds; to come, saying no to a thousand voices that tell us to remain where we are comfortable. It is a call to come away from ourselves. No one who has ever heeded this call will tell you it was in vain.[5]

Through the servitude of parenthood, God unveils our true nature. He reveals moment by moment how to give unconditional love to another. Going to the cradle brings us out of our comfort zone and removes us from the placid stagnation of our own design for our lives. Our plans are a sorry second best for what God has in store for us. In fact, God wants more for us than we can possibly dream.

we caN oNLy ImaɕINe

As we struggle through the difficult and often shocking first few months of motherhood, we sometimes wonder if we can do it. We can't believe one little bundle of joy could be so exhausting. We never knew how much it would change us to be responsible for the life of that tiny creature. If you're like me, you might be amazed—and frankly sometimes even angry—that nobody had told you it would be this hard.

In the latter part of the Old Testament, there is a book written by a prophet named Habakkuk, whose name means "embracer" or "wrestler." The three chapters of this brief book are comprised of dialogue between Habakkuk and God. Habakkuk knew all about difficulties. He was a real person with genuine pain. He wrestled with God over significant heartaches.

> How long, O LORD, must I call for help, but you do not
> listen? Or cry out to you, "Violence!" but you do not save?
> (Habakkuk 1:2)

Our prophet witnessed a medley of atrocities committed by God's people, the Israelites, as well as their enemies. Being a prophet was no picnic. Habakkuk's profession was to be the soothsayer of gloom, doom, and inevitable judgment from God Almighty. What Habakkuk didn't yet realize was that God already had a plan set in motion, and it was a much better plan than Habakkuk could have ever come up with. Finally, God answered his cries:

"Look at the nations and watch—and be utterly amazed.
For I am going to do something in your days that you
would not believe, even if you were told." (1:5)

What an astounding promise to make! "Watch—and be utterly amazed." Over the next several verses, God revealed that His plan was to use the Babylonians, enemies of Israel, to enact judgment upon His people, the Israelites. Although God's plan included judgment and the scattering of His people, the fulfillment of His plan occurred around six hundred years after the death of our perplexed prophet.

Ultimately, God's plan was to give humanity a second chance through His Son, Jesus Christ. Jesus was born in a stable to poor parents. He was placed in a feeding trough surrounded by livestock. His birth was not what many of the Jews had envisioned. God's plan included eternal life through belief in His Son. Justice and judgment are needed; however, God offers mercy and grace to those who will accept it.

Just as our own babies call us away from ourselves, Jesus urges us away from our own self-absorbed worlds. Our Lord calls us away from the busyness of our agendas. He allows difficulties to come into our lives so we can have perspective and so we will once again be dependent upon Him. And He has a plan for our lives that would utterly amaze us.

The problems we face today are much different from the ones Habakkuk encountered. However, Habakkuk was not afraid to bring those problems to God. Let's look to our children and their never-ending needs as opportunities for the Lord to work in our lives in His amazing way. When our burdens become too much for

us and all we see around us is trouble, let's be like Habakkuk, who came forward in all honesty and dumped his load right in front of God. Habakkuk knew that God could handle his questions. He can handle ours as well. God is the same yesterday, today, and forever (see Hebrews 13:8). His reply to us may be the same as the one He gave Habakkuk: "Watch—and be utterly amazed."

I don't know about you, but I'm ready to embrace the lessons God wants to teach me through my babies. I'm tired of complaining and worrying about how hard it can be. I'm ready—truly ready—to be amazed.

CHAPTER 2

THE TODDLER TRENCHES

A family is a unit composed not only of children but of men,
women, an occasional animal, and the common cold.

OGDEN NASH

When I was a little girl, people asked me what I wanted to be when I grew up. Without hesitation, I replied, "I want to be a mom!" with the carefree optimism so prevalent in a healthy, well-adjusted childhood. When asked today, I still answer, "I want to be a mom!" However, it is with experienced and realistic eyes that I respond nowadays. Not getting a good night's sleep for a few years will do that for you.

Being a mom can be exhilarating. There are days I feel as though I am on top of the parental world. Sometimes I am, amazingly enough, completely in sync with my three kids. Discipline issues have been shoved to the dark recesses of my mind and our communication is at a healthy, non-yell pitch. We may even have some inside jokes bantering around. Good grief, on rare occasions they even eat all their dinner. On these mountaintop days, being a

mom is absolutely the best thing in the world!

However, these are not the days we like to hear about from other parents (if we're honest with ourselves). The things that are fun to read and laugh about are other people's kerfuffles with their children: the goof-ups, foibles, quandaries, confusions, mistakes, and general problems that come with the territory. In our gut, we need confirmation that other people also fight like cats and dogs all the way to church. (Note: The word *kerfuffle* is actually in the dictionary and means "disorder or commotion."[6] I learned it from the character Marilla Cuthbert in the movie *Anne of Green Gables*, and I have adopted it as one of my own. Feel free to borrow it as often as you like; it's quite descriptive in a pinch.)

We've had plenty of kerfuffles in our home, with several looming up ahead (I refer you to chapter 10, "Where Can I Get a Fast Pass Through the Teen Years?"). The beauty is that being open and honest about our difficulties not only relieves our friends (who, for some strange reason, think we have it all together) but also helps reveal areas in which the Lord desires to mold and change us toward becoming more like Himself.

My children's toddler years were for me a time of desperate reliance upon my heavenly Father. Gosh, the mothers on television always made it look so easy—boy, was I fooled. For those of us living in the real world, being a mom in the toddler trenches can be excruciatingly difficult at times. The possibility of dying of a laundry overdose seems not only feasible but also morbidly inevitable. So does the likelihood of drowning in a sea of dishes—or ketchup. As toddlers, my children discovered the culinary usefulness of that blessed pureed tomato sauce. They still love it. They will eat any kind of meat product as long as it is splashed with a generous

amount of Heinz. I figure that between ketchup and applesauce, we're in good shape on the food pyramid.

you've come a Long way, baby

How about Amoxicillin? The toddler years often made me feel like I was drowning in a pink sea of antibiotics. There was a time when our children were sick and I was coming down with it as well. We had been to the doctor's office and were making the sojourn to the pharmacy for—you guessed it—Amoxicillin. I hadn't slept in several days (or was it months? I can't remember). Being the mother of toddlers, the only showers I encountered on any regular basis were the kind that had lousy games and, with any luck, good cake. Makeup wasn't something I put on my face; rather, it was something my husband and I needed to do quite frequently, particularly when he mentioned anything about my apparent lack of makeup and showers.

As I lugged my beloved offspring to the back of the pharmacy, I was somewhat self-conscious about the dried baby spit-up on my left shoulder (soon to be joined by my right shoulder). Because I was still nursing, I was wearing my oh-so-feminine nursing bra, complete with those little coaster-shaped nursing pads that made my chest look like giant felt-tip markers.

The tough thing about pharmacies is that the medicines you work so hard at keeping out of your children's reach at home are conveniently located at shin level. My husband tells me it's a marketing thing. And they're in those colorful boxes, to boot. The day we were stranded at the pharmacy was the day I realized one puzzle in the waiting room simply was not enough to hold my kids' attention.

I got quite a workout that day. From the hemorrhoid creams to the birth control devices, the enticing array of medications beckoned to my children like honey to Winnie the Pooh. It took every ounce of raw maternal energy I had to keep those shelves restocked in their original order. Ten minutes turned to twenty; twenty turned to twenty-five. Just as I considered the option of administering an assortment of random leftover prescriptions from the medicine cabinet at home, I was called forth by Miss Perky.

The pharmacist on duty that day looked perky, dressed perky, smiled perky, and talked perky. You get the picture. Not feeling the least bit perky myself, I found it rather nauseating. While I had been busily re-shelving, Miss Perky had been gushing about her upcoming trip to the Bahamas with her "gorgeous boyfriend." This little gal was cute, intelligent, sophisticated, and had everyone in the entire pharmacy listening attentively to every perky word that came out of her mouth. As I was summoned to the counter, she bent down from her lofty pharmaceutical throne to explain the directions on how to administer Amoxicillin (three times a day for ten days . . .). It was at this moment that I made the decision to clear up a few possible misunderstandings on her part.

"Excuse me, I just wanted to say that I haven't always looked like this. I used to shower on a regular basis. I even dressed in style. I actually went to college and graduated on the dean's list with a bachelor of arts degree in psychology. I have been known in the past to hold somewhat interesting and stimulating conversations. I've even been described as 'perky.' Just thought you'd like to know."

She gazed at me impassively, raised those perky little eyebrows at me, and said, "Okay, now, remember to refrigerate and use up all the medication in a ten-day period. Buh-bye!"

By the way, the word on the street is that this particular pharmacist has since gotten married to Mr. Bahamas and has produced a couple of Amoxicillin-bound babies. The next time we meet, I may feel compelled to break out singing, "I love you, you love me, we're a happy family. . . ."

Locker Room Levitation

One way to combat those pesky flu germs is to antibacterialize them. You know what I'm talking about: Costco-size antibacterial soap. Personally, I call myself a germaphobic. I have issues with things like sharing sodas and toothbrushes. After having questioned dozens of our friends on this subject, it appears that I am the sole individual on the planet who would choose fuzzy teeth over using my spouse's toothbrush. Go figure.

The camping experience is in itself quite a stretch for a germaphobic. On one camping trip in particular, right in the middle of my antibacterial prime, our children were three and two years old. Because we were camping in the Northwest, it was, of course, raining. We had decided to forgo the local waterslides in lieu of a nearby indoor swimming pool. When we were finished with the swimming thing, we traipsed into the family locker room (translation: closet-size room with a showerhead, drain, potty, and sink).

Now, I don't know about the rest of you, but there's something about cold water on cold yellow tile (complete with a few old Band-Aids and hair remnants thrown in for good measure) that enables me to come as close to levitation as humanly possible. I can pretty much walk on the tips of my big toenails. So there I was, levitating on my toenails and getting my two kids antibacterialized for

the campground. I had just finished with J.J., the three-year old, and given him the express instruction to "stay put and don't touch *anything*!"

I began vigorously scrubbing our two-year-old, Katie. Midway through the purification process, I happened to look up at my sanitized son. To my shock and absolute horror, he was crouched on the ground over the shower drain scooping the water in a little circle. It was an echo-y room and I could hear myself saying, "J.J., now J.J. You need to stop, J.J.—that's dirty water. Now honey. Icky icky icky." While in mid-nag, he looked up at me, made eye contact, and in slow motion went, "Ssllluuurrrppp!"

Yes, he drank that shower-drain water, cooties and all. It was pretty much an out-of-body experience for me. I screamed, "No!" with all the melodramatic flair I could muster at the time. I didn't know what to do to him—or for him. My considerations were Tevye-like, reminiscent of the poor indecisive father from *Fiddler on the Roof*: *On the one hand, Ipecac will induce vomiting, which I don't want to deal with on this floor. On the other hand, bleach may do more internal damage than any germ critter could ever do.*

As I sorted through the solutions at hand, my husband came running in looking wild-eyed as he tried to ascertain exactly which limb had been cut off. You can be assured that when the ruckus subsided, I made sure to scrub that kid from lips to toes. You never saw a camping kid looking so clean. I must admit that I wasn't able to conjure up the will to kiss him anywhere near the lips for a very, very long time. To this day, years later, an occasional unknown virus will crop up and I'll worry and wonder if there could still be any lingering effects from his little sip from the shower.

mommy worries

There are times when my "mommy worries" completely catch me off guard. I am sorry to admit the bald-faced truth that prior to getting married, all I worried about was myself. What can I say, I'm a Gen Xer. After our wedding day, I occasionally worried a bit about my new husband. However, the day I found out I was pregnant with baby number one was a day that shall live in infamy. It was the day the worry gland exploded into existence in my being (sort of like the Big Bang Theory) and gradually evolved to monstrous proportions. I'll never live down the phone call I made to my brother-in-law, the cardiologist of the family: "Joe, I'm pregnant, and I've been using eyedrops for the last month. Do you think my baby is okay?"

Apparently, saline solution eyedrops are harmless. Who knew? My husband is not a worrier in the least. His name is Ben. Ben and Jenn. We rhyme. We are nothing alike. He graduated with a degree in business and marketing. I graduated from a small Christian university with a degree in psychology and a concentration in human services. To sum it up: I'm mushy and he's not.

Remember the load of Amoxicillin consumption? Our two older children had finally polished off their final gallon when our doctor prescribed ear tubes for both of them. They were one and two years old. Although ear tube surgery is a fairly safe procedure, I was supremely concerned about my babies being put under anesthesia and not coming back out!

Ben characteristically took the whole thing in stride, though, even when we had to show up at the hospital with our two-year-old at 6:30 a.m. to prepare for surgery. As the morning passed, I could feel the mommy jitters creeping into my heart. The nurse entered

the room prior to his surgery and administered some spiked juice to him (they weren't offering any to me, unfortunately). After he was pretty much out of it, they wheeled in an enormous crib on wheels and placed him in it, Elmo hospital gown and all. If you have busy children at home, you understand how unsettling it is to see them lying completely still during the day.

The physician approached carrying a tower of notebooks with him. Oddly enough, I remember thinking at the time, *Good grief, isn't he supposed to have all this stuff memorized? The last thing I want to picture is him looking frantically for the paragraph on "How to wake the kid up"!*

After informing us of all the risks (eeek!) and concerns involved with our child's procedure, he looked us both in the eye and asked if we had any particular questions he could answer for us. I felt my throat constrict; it was all I could do not to cry in front of him. J.J. was lying there looking so helpless and, well, still. I had been told I wouldn't be able to come into the surgery area but would have to wait in another room (on another floor, for Pete's sake). I shook my head. I couldn't think of any new questions. I certainly wasn't going to start blubbering right in front of Dr. Notebooks. He needed to be able to focus on my inebriated offspring with the bad ears. Ben said quietly, "I have a question." I mentally high-fived him: *Good for you, hon!* The doctor gripped his manuals, ready to look something up, and I held my breath as we both leaned in to hear what Ben had to say: "While he's in surgery, will I have time to go get some breakfast?" *That* was his question. He was having some rumblies in his tumbly at a time like this. The doctor paused a moment with a strange look on his face and answered, "Well, I wouldn't leave the building."

I was mortified. I'm sure he pictured Ben cruising down to Denny's for a Grand Slam breakfast as soon as our boy was wheeled away. However, Ben knew something the medical staff didn't: I was going to worry enough that day for both of us—no reason for both of us to go hungry.

a JOURNEY FOR JOY

I was knee-deep in the toddler trenches. I had a two-year-old who was still getting up four to five times a night, a three-year-old who was having some killer tantrums, and baby number three on the way. It got to the point that we felt the need to ask our parents for their advice. We figured they had some experience here; surely they'll know what to do. My mom is a sweet pushover who raised three shy, compliant, obedient little girls (oh, how the memory goes with time). When presented with the problem, she answered like any good mother would, "You're being too hard on him. It's your fault he's having a tough time. What are you doing to make him scream and cry like that? You just need to love him more. Just love him through the tough times."

Gag, I know. Needless to say, we tried "loving him through the tough times," and it seemed to get worse. So we went to Ben's mom. Ben's mom, incidentally, had five children in a five-and-half-year time period. Let's have a moment of silence for Ben's mom. . . . Okay, moving on. Four of her five kids were (um, and still are) active, strong-willed little boys. She too had some advice for us: "Fill a glass with water and then throw it in his face!" I freaked out when she suggested it. However, I eventually got to that point again and, well, just so you know, water in the face works.

Okay, back to the trenches. I was underslept, overworked, and feeling totally unappreciated by my little cherubs. I'm sure this story sounds vaguely familiar to some of you. My social life was limited to the nursery at church and the checkout line at Safeway. I was convinced I was losing brain cells at an alarming rate.

On a particular Monday (laundry and bathroom cleaning day), I lay in bed, dreading the week, unable to drum up the gumption to get moving. The upcoming five days loomed over my head, and I felt as though I would be crushed by the sheer weight of caregiving responsibilities. I began to pray (okay, whine is more accurate) to God: "Lord, why did you give me the desire to do this? Why is this my life's calling? I know this is what you created me for, but why this? I could have been better used in something more important, more recognized, more glamorous, better paid. Why are we wasting all this potential? I could have been a teacher, a musician, a lawyer, a perky pharmacist—anything but this!"

Right in the middle of my prayer, I recalled a challenge issued by my teaching leader at Bible Study Fellowship. Our teacher had urged us to pray each morning specifically for God to fill us up with His joy. What a concept! I'd been a Christian since childhood, and I'd never prayed for God to fill me with His joy. So I prayed, "God, help me to have joy today in the middle of all this. I don't feel any joy in what I'm doing for you, and I truly desire it."

I grumpily dragged myself out of bed (my husband says that's the *only* way I know how to get out of bed). We began the morning routine with breakfast and a movie. Our kids chose a Mr. Rogers video we had checked out from the library. It was yet unwatched, so it was going to be a perfect attention-getter. My day was already looking better.

This particular episode was about nametags. We learned more about nametags than I thought possible. Our son, J.J., watched in a semi-comatose state as Mr. Rogers made nametags for all his friends. And then he made one for us, his television friends. However, because he didn't know our names, Mr. Rogers carefully wrote out the word "YOU." Well, to say the least, this intrigued J.J. He wanted to make nametags like Mr. Rogers all day! He wanted to make some for all his friends and family and neighbors, so we got to work. I did the cutting, and he did the writing. He made stacks of those nametags, each one color-coordinated and individually designed. I taped several on J.J.'s shirt, and Katie and I were each wearing our own custom-designed "YOU" nametag.

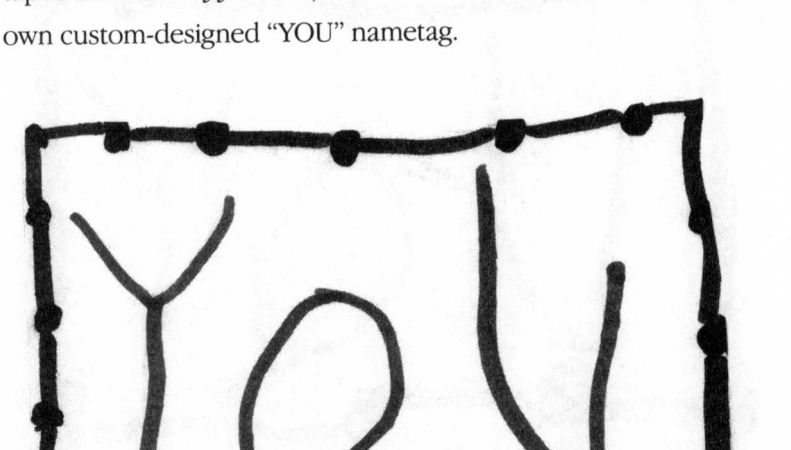

All throughout the day I kept praying, "God, please give me Your joy; I'm sick to death of these nametags!" Later that day, I was upstairs cleaning out the bathroom sink. From the back room, I heard my kiddos fighting (yet again) over their toys. I felt the

heaviness and discomfort of my third pregnancy. And then I wondered how many months it would take before our newest addition would be screaming at her siblings and launching Legos out of her crib. I closed my eyes and looked into the sink as I came before the Lord. I felt defeated, rundown, and utterly joyless.

"Please Lord, Your joy is all I am asking for. Obedience to the call would be so much easier if I knew you approved of what I am doing here." When I finally looked up with tears in my eyes, it was a wondrous sight that I beheld in the mirror:

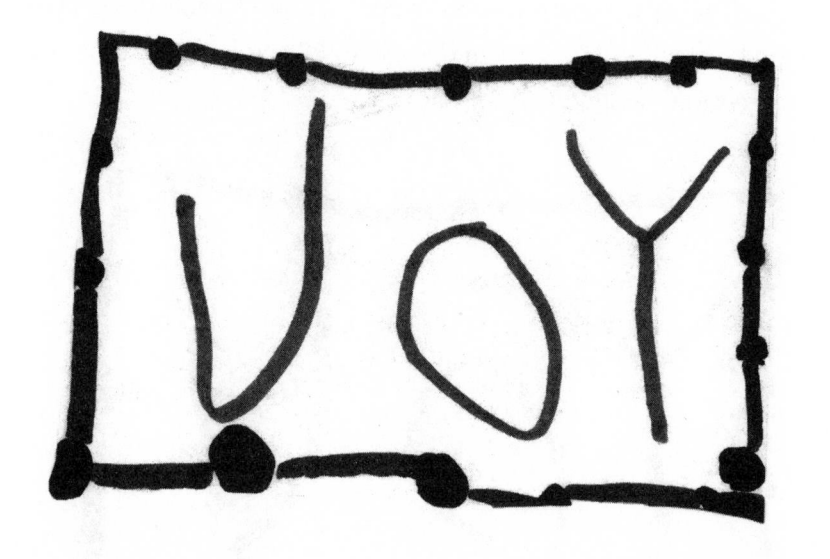

The three-year-old with whom I had been so frustrated had been used by God that day in a most awesome and unexpected way. J.J.'s little hand had been guided by the Father in writing out the word "YOU" so that in the mirror it clearly read "JOY" to my sorely sapped soul. God had heard the depths of my prayers. Even though I complained and whined to Him, He didn't reprimand or discipline me. Rather, He chose to answer and bless me through

the very child with whom I was so irritated. I didn't deserve such a gift from Him.

Maybe that's why I was so moved by it. Through this small miracle, I heard Him say to me, "Dear child, I love you and know what you are going through. This is indeed the calling I have for you, and I am never wrong. Trust Me to get you through victoriously and joyfully. Rely on My strength and not your own. Focus on Me and not on yourself. I am with you now and will be with you always."

I taped the nametag in my Bible to remind me of the day God showed me the source of true joy: Himself. The message continues to bless and reach out to me. It reminds me of God's eternal sovereignty and strength. During the trench years, His joy had appeared to be something I could never attain. I had been looking for joy in the wrong places. I was searching for specific feelings (unhindered happiness, the thrill of accomplishment) and physical manifestations of achievement (a clean house, well-behaved children, manicured toes). In themselves, these are not bad things to strive for; however, I realized that the joy God offers to me is not dependent upon any level of success in my estimation. Underneath the nametag, I have written, "The joy of the Lord is your strength" (Nehemiah 8:10).

God didn't give me fluffy emotions that day, nor did He radically change my circumstances. Every Monday I'm still knee-deep in laundry and pink-rimmed toilets that need to meet Mr. Clean and Mrs. Scrub brush. God chose to help me within the confines of my toil rather than by waving a magic wand over my head. In essence, God reached down to my heart and reminded me of a wonderful truth and admonition: "The LORD is my strength and my song; he has become my salvation. He is my God, and I will praise him, my

father's God, and I will exalt him" (Exodus 15:2).

Another beautiful and surprising aspect of the joy story is that it provided me with a wonderful anecdote to share with my friends. Over the years, I have shared it with dozens of people. Then I was asked to tell it from the pulpit at church on Mother's Day. I couldn't believe the rush I experienced from watching the faces before me transform from laughter to understanding to restoration. God was using me (me!) to reach out and comfort other women.

I soon found myself speaking at local MOPS (Mothers of Preschoolers) groups. Finally, after a year of prayerful searching, I approached my husband with the unthinkable: I wanted to write a book. How lofty that sounded to my housekeeping ears! And yet it had been a secret wish of mine for years. Ben didn't think it lofty at all. In fact, he thought it to be the most obvious direction for my life. His encouragement and faith propelled me to take the first steps toward publication. And the rest, as they say, is history.

My heavenly Father caressed my heart with the comfort only He can bring when He spoke through the nametags. He also gave me a purpose and fulfilled a dream that had been tucked into the deepest part of my soul. The joy of the Lord is a thread I have woven throughout this book. The fact that God can and does use each person to minister to one another continues to amaze and inspire me. So read on, laundry-laden ladies. The joy of the Lord is your strength!

CHAPTER 3

ReaL moms
DON'T NeeD PLUNGeRS

One year, I'd completely lost my bearings trying to follow potty training instruction from a psychiatric expert. I was stuck on step one, which stated without an atom of irony: "Before you begin, remove all stubbornness from the child." I knew it only could have been written by someone whose suit coat was still spotless at the end of the day, not someone who had any hands-on experience with an actual two-year-old.

MARY KAY BLAKELY

A Real mom:

1. Carries baby wipes and antibacterial gel in her purse
2. Utilizes handy phrases her own mother used (for example: "Because I said so!")
3. Thinks of minivans as God's gift to humankind
4. Gets a thrill when Kraft mac and cheese goes on sale
5. Occasionally locks herself in the bathroom to have a decent phone conversation

I know that this chapter's title is a little on the edge. However, I think it gets to the bowels of motherhood, the *real* stuff that makes up a large part of our daily existence: poo-poo and potty. I can't

possibly be the only mother who has inadvertently asked the adults within range if they need to go potty.

The poo-poo inundation began the day we came home from the hospital. As we prepared for checkout, the nurse hurriedly ran through the color checklist. Still reeling from a medicated hang-over, I had trouble keeping up with her.

"Wait, which color should it start out as?"

"Black. Oh, and it should be the consistency of tar."

Tar? Who checks for bowel consistency?

"Then green. It must go from black to green. And it will be more like thick toothpaste."

Gross. "It must? What do I do if it doesn't?"

"Then yellow. It should look a lot like mustard."

Great. So much for ever using that condiment again.

She briskly concluded with the grand finale: "Brown. In a few months, when he starts eating real foods, then it should be brown."

Grimace.

We drove away and waved at her on the curb, the colors and consistencies swirling through our heads.

"Oh," she called out ominously, "if it turns red at any time, you need to call the hospital right away—that's bad!"

So I rehearsed all the way home: "Black tar, green toothpaste, yellow mustard, brown. . . . Hey, Ben, I can't remember: Was it black toothpaste or black tar?"

tHe cIRCLe of LIfe

If you want to know what defines the type of mom you are, I have two words for you: cloth diapers. Back in my babysitting

prime, cloth diapering was the norm rather than the exception. I remember trying to hold down those wiggly little bodies, the pin poised precariously over the fold. I broke out in a sweat every time. Someone was going to get poked—either the baby or me. Then I had to rinse the dirty one out in the toilet, let it soak for awhile, and then re-rinse it. Finally it had to be wrung out and stored in the diaper pail, where it waited to be washed, bleached, and rewashed before being reused.

These are the memories that propelled me to make the politically incorrect, environmentally unfriendly decision to go with disposable. There are some things I am not willing to endure for Mother Earth. She can just start decomposing the little suckers. I'm told the decomposition process should go from light brown, to green, and conclude with a black substance, something akin to tar.

you've come a Long way, Baby

When our children were newborns, every trip to the grocery store included an extra large package of whatever diaper happened to be on sale, each package clearly revealing the weight and size of the target market. This helpful information lets parents know when it's time to graduate their child's tush to the next incremental size on the box.

We had our own system. Ben and I always knew when the baby was ready to progress to the next-size diaper when we'd experience an up-the-back dilemma (aka blowout). This was an especially unpleasant occurrence when it happened at the outset of an extended car trip. By the time we realized the up-the-back special had transpired, the baby's undershirt was glued to his backside. Nothing short

of a lengthy scrub-down would remove the encrusted garment. It was such a freeing moment when our youngest child had a blowout and we could simply throw her clothes away!

Then there's the fun that takes place in the bathroom. At the age of two, each of our children performed what we call the Toddler TP Rite of Passage. Unable to resist the urge to unroll and wad up an entire roll of toilet paper, my children successfully completed each ceremony by shoving the whole bundle down the toilet. I think what they were really after was the waterfall effect following the flush. During the toddler years, we owned one plunger and three toilets. (We've since learned our lesson—we now own one plunger per potty.) There were a number of times I couldn't find or reach the plunger. This may (or may not) come as a shock to you, but I have been known to, well, use my hand in a moment of desperation. Please, gentle reader, suppress your judgment until you've heard my rationalization: It's not like I haven't already been up to my elbows in those germs since their birth! (For any of you who are squeamish, I apologize. But honestly, haven't you been in a similarly revolting situation at some point in your mommy career?)

Then there's potty training. Need I say more? Being in the potty-training stage is like traveling to the Twilight Zone. The child progresses and then digresses. He's trained; he's not trained. And through the entire process, you've changed your tactics so many times that you can't remember if you're supposed to give them candy or money or a spanking when they actually go in the toilet.

When our last child turned three, Ben and I experienced an unusual urgency in our potty-training lessons. "Think of how much money we'll save each month!" we gleefully anticipated. We could see the end of our diaper-changing tunnel and were sprinting toward

the light. In retrospect, we may have been hitting the potty-training sessions a little too hard. Poor Emma began showing signs of potty-training paranoia. Any adult who crossed her path was looked upon suspiciously as a possible underwear undercover agent.

One night at a church function, a few leaders were on hand to help supervise our roaming rascals. In the middle of a game of dodgeball, our little Emma plopped down on the floor next to one of the helpers. His only child happened to be in the fifth grade at the time, so potty training was but a faint memory. Emma took one look at him, realized he was a parental figure, and jumped to the (incorrect) conclusion that it was his turn for potty-training patrol. Completely catching him off guard, Miss Emma looked him right in the eye and pronounced, "I won't be stayin' and I won't be takin' off my panties!" Needless to say, he was speechless.

the test

As mothers facing the never-ending reality of embarrassing and unpleasant bathroom issues, the yearly female exam is an additional benefit, sort of like an end-of-the-year bonus. My mom refers to this appointment as the torture chamber. The week prior to my appointment never fails to be anything short of total disaster. By the time I get into the car for my first moments of peace since last year's appointment, I think of the upcoming exam and proclaim, "Fine, bring it on!"

It's amazing how quickly our gynecological clocks tick. We go through the year, oblivious to the monthly countdown. Then the reminder card comes. Time never seems to pass as quickly as when we need to make the appointment for our annual pelvic exam.

Didn't I just do *this?* we ask ourselves.

However, we live in the days of medical prevention, so we grudgingly parcel out the kids and prepare to spend our morning off with the gynecologist and a two-year-old issue of *People* magazine. The visit doesn't start out well; it always commences with the weigh-in. For some reason, the scale at the doctor's office is always at least ten pounds heavier than the one at home. I even take off my shoes, purse, keys, and coat to lighten things up (this never works). During the weigh-in at my last appointment, the nurse watched me de-layering. When I took off my socks, she chuckled and said, "Everyone does that." I think they should give us a break every now and then. Oh, how fun it would be to breeze past the scales and a sign that says, "Weigh Station Closed."

After we're rudely confronted with our accurate weight, the nurse then transports us to the nearest ice cold room and dangles a skimpy gown at us before heading off to the next weigh-in victim. The fluttering gown is somewhat like the waving of the black-and-white flag prior to a NASCAR event. Once the door closes, it's a race against time. It's bad enough to be seen clutching the threadbare gown (does the tie go in the front or the back?), but to be caught midway through undressing, well, that would be too much. Then there's the panty/bra disappearing act. We try as hard as we can to roll those things into a ball and hide them under our clothes. What, like they'll think we don't wear them?

Then there's The Clamp. I don't know its correct medical term (nor do I want to, for that matter); I've just always referred to it as The Clamp. Back when I had my first female exam, I was ushered into the room (following the weigh-in) and did a quick-change that would have put Superman to shame. The nurse came back and

slammed an enormous metal thing down on the counter next to where I was sitting. She briskly informed me the doctor would be right in. *Okay, fine*, I thought nervously, *but what in the world is that thing for?* I soon found out.

There are two times I pray specifically for God not to send an earthquake. One is when I'm driving through the Alaskan Way viaduct in Seattle. Whenever I go through those yellow tunnels, I do some serious conversing with the Lord. The other time is when I'm in The Clamp. I can't imagine how in the world I could get out of that thing on my own in an emergency.

"So, let's hop up on the table. Okay, now scoot a little closer, scoot, scoot, almost. Okay, a little closer. Relax your knees, scoot, relax, scoot, relax, scoot, okay. This is going to be a little (a LITTLE?) cold; you'll feel a little bit of pressure." All of a sudden, the serious, all-business doctor turns into Chatty Cathy. "So, what's been going on in your household lately? Have you been enjoying any new hobbies?" At this point my mind is a complete blank. *Hobbies? What are those? Household? Do I have one?* The only thing that registers is that I've seen that Garfield poster somewhere before but can't quite put my finger on it. Oh, yeah, at the dentist's office — my other favorite place to go on my day off.

the real mom

Besides the reality of never-ending sticky doorknobs and rare moments of privacy, Real moms have real hurts, real frustrations, and real weaknesses. Too often we think the gal sitting next to us has this "mom thing" figured out so much more than we do. We're wrong, of course. She has her own issues. The realities of marriage

struggles, physical problems, parenting issues, and maybe even the loss of a loved one can strike anyone at any time. And it's during these times when our insecurities rise to the surface, taunting us and our self-congratulatory moments of success.

Case in point: About thirteen years ago, I experienced my first panic attack. Strangely enough, it was on our honeymoon (poor, poor Ben). It's difficult to express the depth of uncertainty and fear I encountered. In fact, the whole situation took my breath away with its unexpected control over my sense of well-being and confidence.

After a few years, I found a doctor who identified the problem. Oh, how I wrestled with his conclusion! Panic attacks are not scientifically measurable. They are not tangible to anyone outside their grip. There is no honor in suffering through a panic attack. What a humbling diagnosis for me, a person who felt she could conquer the world (one plunger at a time).

Over the past decade, I have been able to set aside my pride a little, trust the Lord more, and finally accept the diagnosis. In fact, I've experienced panic attacks sporadically ever since. During the early years, I would tell myself, *I am not the kind of person to whom these things happen. People who experience panic attacks are fearful and weak and not trusting in God, right?* I couldn't have been more wrong. The reality is that we all experience stress, pain, disappointments, and suffering.

However, when we look at the world around us, it is difficult to determine what, exactly, is expected of us. Our media and our culture seem to tell us that nothing less than perfection is acceptable—perfectly clean house, perfectly behaved children, perfectly manicured nails. Anything short of this can make us feel like

failures. We spend so much of our time comparing ourselves to others, trying to measure up to the impossible standard of perfection—especially television perfection.

Who is it that we most identify with? Who are we trying to imitate? Our own mothers may have fancied Lucy Ricardo or Carol Brady. How about those of us living in the modern world? Martha Stewart? Gosh, even her name makes her seem cool, in control:

"Good morning ladies. I am here to show you a wonderfully simple Friday-night meal you can prepare for your family with a touch of creativity and preparation. It will be delicious, healthy, and, of course, attractive to look at. I'm sure you're all familiar with Macaroni and Cheese. Well, we are going to be making our own cheese today for our main dish. Children love assisting with this, and it's so helpful to have them in the kitchen, isn't it? Fresh home-made bread will accompany our pasta dish along with some freshly squeezed apple cider followed by carrots shaped into miniature swing sets. Remember: It's the details that make every meal all the more special. Later we'll be creating centerpiece menus with pictures of our children cut out and glued around the periphery of the menu."

As if! I mean, who can possibly look that efficient and capable and put-together and *calm* all the time? It helps me to picture a host of Martha Stewart's assistants, ranging from dish washers to makeup artists, hovering nearby.

There's another Martha I've admired and have learned from over the years. Pieces of her life are recorded in the book of Luke in the New Testament. Martha had a sister named Mary. These gals weren't even remotely as put-together as Martha Stewart. They had strengths as well as weaknesses. They were gifted women trying

their best to serve the Lord and others around them. One of them allowed her service to distract her from what was truly important (something that happens to the best of us!).

Mary and Martha also had a brother named Lazarus. The three of them were friends of Jesus and had spent a lot of time with Him at their home. In Luke 10, Martha invites Jesus and His disciples to come and stay with them:

> As Jesus and his disciples were on their way, he came to a village where a woman named Martha opened her home to him. She had a sister called Mary, who sat at the Lord's feet listening to what he said. But Martha was distracted by all the preparations that had to be made. She came to him and asked, "Lord, don't you care that my sister has left me to do the work by myself? Tell her to help me!" (verses 38-40)

If you find this Mary-and-Martha story familiar, you might have the same opinion that I do: Poor Martha has been given the shaft. Over the years, commentaries and Bible teachers have specifically honed in on two aspects of these two women: Mary's wonderfulness and Martha's whininess. I'd like to look a little closer at Martha. She's the one most of us can relate to.

Many scholars agree that Martha was more than likely the eldest child in her family.[7] (I am the eldest as well!) Because she was the one who invited Jesus and Company, it is safe to assume that the home belonged to her. We can infer that because she was a woman in that day who owned a home, she was responsible, resourceful, industrious, and smart. She seemed willing to share with others and

help Jesus and His disciples. Clearly, her love language was hospitality. She invited everyone in and welcomed them to her table. (I
can relate to this! I love helping people out; I love serving people; I
love cooking food for people.) It's easy to picture Martha with her
Hebrew apron on as she stood on her porch ushering her guests
into the house. I wish I could go back in time and watch this firsthand: the room overflowing with visitors, cushions gathered from
all corners of the house, food hauled out of the fridge (or whatever),
extra dinnerware set out for the guests. Martha is in her element!
For the time being, she is the hero of the night.

However, the Bible says that over the course of the night, Martha
became distracted by all of the preparations. (I can relate to that
too!) She was frustrated because even though she willingly offered
to feed and clean up after all these men, doggone it, they were
messy, messy, messy. They had eaten a ton of her food. Apparently,
no one had made a move to help her, and then her little sister had
the nerve to plant herself among the men as they listened to Jesus.
I usually mutter to myself when I'm ticked off. Martha seems like a
mutterer. Were we to listen carefully, we might have heard something like this: "Who does Mary think she is? She's supposed to be
helping me out! Here I am doing all the work by myself!" (Okay,
now I'm starting to get a little uncomfortable in this comparison
thing. Maybe I can relate a little too much to Martha.) But Jesus
looked at her and said, "Martha, Martha, [Doesn't that sound sweet?
He gently calmed her down.] . . . you are worried and upset about
many things, but only one thing is needed. Mary has chosen what is
better, and it will not be taken away from her" (Luke 10:41-42).

Jesus knew she was worried and upset. He basically said to her,
"Hey, I know things are not going exactly how you want them to go.

You are out of control of the situation, and you hate it! However, your sister has chosen to listen to Me, and that is more important than the details you are so anxious about."

Martha forgot the whole reason she volunteered her home in the first place: to take care of Jesus so He could teach and train others. Now, let's not be too hard on her; Jesus wasn't. We can see how it happened. She meant good but allowed her own frustrations to get in the way.

In many ways, I want to be like Martha. I want to be responsible, hardworking, sharing, caring, and willing to minister. I want to be the first one on the scene to offer hospitality and friendship. Jesus reminded Martha that although what she was doing was valuable and important, there was only one thing that was truly needed: to listen to Jesus' teachings. Notice that Jesus didn't rebuke Martha when she was serving with a giving heart. He reached out to her when her attitude got stinky. What she received from Jesus was a strong dose of encouragement and a refresher on her priorities. We all need that, don't we?

Sometimes as moms we work ourselves into a frenzy just trying to get the stuff done that needs to be done. The distractions of plungers, potty training, and pelvic exams absorb so much of our time and energy. We need to stop and look around. We need to temporarily set aside the burdens we carry from day to day. We need to listen to Jesus. "Jenn, Jenn, you are worried and upset about many things, but only one thing is needed. Mary has chosen what is better, and it will not be taken away from her."

I want to be like Mary too—to be the one who has chosen what is better. I want to know that He will be pleased by my choice, and I want the reassurance that it will not be taken away from me.

These are the ladies I want to look up to, admire, relate to, and learn from.

As mothers let's not let the stinky realities of life cloud the reality of God. It's fun and therapeutic to laugh together about some of the hilarious scenes we deal with as moms. However, I would also like to give you a dose of encouragement and help you get a better handle on the priorities in your life. Remember our two sisters, remember they were not perfect, and remember the words Jesus said to them (and to us):

"Dear one, do not be worried and upset about so many things. Choose what is better. Choose Me. And I promise: No one can ever take Me away from you."

A Real mom:

1. Loves her kids in spite of all the stickiness
2. Makes mistakes and experiences pain and suffering
3. Knows that she is loved and accepted by a very Real God

H O U D I N I   W H O ?

Speech is conveniently located midway between thought and action, where it often substitutes for both.

John Andrew Holmes

People always laugh when we tell them that all our furniture is bolted to the walls. Then they see our sober expressions and notice the skid marks halfway up the wall. Yup, busy, busy, busy. At one point, we were the proud owners of six baby gates. We were a true "gated community."

The fact is, our kids were all born with the proverbial fire-crackers in their pants. They're here, they're there—they're everywhere I *don't* want them to be! They are walking, jumping, climbing "anti–Visa ads" ("Visa—it's everywhere you want to be"). It's exhausting being with them. They are my greatest treasures in life and my greatest frustrations and the source of most of my humor—okay, *all* of my humor.

And you have to laugh when you live in a house where you have to hop over three gates and mangle your finger in the childproofed

latches in order to get an extra roll of toilet paper. I don't think my fingernails will ever recover from the years of removing outlet plugs. Gates, locks, plugs. During the toddler years, my entire life was one big plastic obstacle course.

The only person in the family who could successfully open those cupboard latches was our two-and-a-half-year-old, Katie. She made Houdini look plain wimpy in comparison. One morning she managed to open the "locked" cupboard and drink down half a bottle of Dawn dish detergent. I know it was half a bottle because while I was on the phone with Poison Control (yet again), I witnessed the entire capacity, in all its blue glory, vault out of her mouth and onto our carpet. "The human body is an amazing thing," the Poison Control expert informed me. Yep, pretty amazing.

Many years ago I started counting to three during my kids' naughty moments before the inevitable disciplinary action took place. I know I am not alone in this counting thing; in fact, I thought it rather dopey before I was a mom (ah, the things we think we know before experience kicks in). However, now I realize this counting business is not just for *their* benefit. An innocent bystander, whose child was only an infant at the time, witnessed one of my counting episodes and offered the following advice: "You know, you should really expect them to obey the first time and not at the count of three."

Oh, I expect them to obey before I count to three. I start counting so I don't physically explode! I'd count to ten, but I don't have that kind of time. You see, in a flash they'll be on to some new place of terror, wherever the firecrackers lead them. We moms use the tools God gives in order to survive, do we not? If counting to three keeps me from an all-out mommy temper tantrum, then hallelujah: "1, 2, 3!" I'm not talking about lowering our standards—just tweaking them a bit.

cAuTION: CHILDReN at pLay!

We knew that our first child, J.J., was busy. He was crawling everywhere by seven months and sprinting by twelve months. However, nothing prepared us for our second little sweetie pie, Katie (who, by the way, was sprinting by nine months). When she was one year old, she repeatedly climbed up on her second-story window ledge and tried to open the window. Her favorite pastime was perching on the tops of tables, counters, dressers, balcony ledges—you name it. If it produced a mild stroke for any adults in range, she climbed it.

Some friends of ours have three "anti–Visa ad" children as well. They're all boys age five and under and apparently a little accident-prone. In fact, recently the entire family spent four weekends in a row at three different emergency rooms. Sandwiched between visits to their own local hospital were two trips to hospitals in cities where they were vacationing. I've summarized the collective diagnoses: (1) broken arm for kid number one, (2) stitches from falling onto a Lego in the middle of the night for kid number two, (3) curling iron burn for kid number three, (4) forehead stitches from falling on the fireplace for kid number one again. And in between all this, Mom had to go to the hospital for a slipped disk she incurred most likely from hauling kids into the ER! Their adorable kids definitely love life and spend a lot of time trying to experience as much as possible before naptime. If you spend even five minutes with this family, you will realize how miraculous it is that they're all still alive and functional. It's pretty sad, though, when you're on a first-name basis with the local hospital staff.

As we get older, it's difficult to remember the sensation of

having that much energy, enthusiasm, and excitement for life. Too often we face each day with an attitude of mature mediocrity rather than childlike zip and zest. We are so concerned with the watering, fertilizing, and trimming that we forget to smell the roses.

when you're ready, you're ready

There's nothing like the smell of a new school year. New clothes, new backpacks, new glue sticks, falling leaves, and getting up early. Two years ago, my husband and I experienced our first back-to-school moment since our own school days. It was time for J.J. to start kindergarten. Although I had been mentally preparing myself for six and a half years, putting my oldest child on that great big school bus was not a test for the faint of heart. It seemed that on the walk from our front door to the bus stop, our son had shrunk to about half his size. The sixth-graders were enormous next to him. After giving me one last "Help!" look, he hoisted his backpack onto his slim little shoulders and scrambled onto the bus. My tears in check, I proudly waved to him and then raced off to my van and followed him all the way to school sobbing my heart out.

My girlfriend, however, wasn't quite ready to put her kid on the bus under the care of a complete stranger, so she decided to drive him to school for his first year. That lasted about a week. He too was a six-year-old kindergartner, and he felt the need to grow up a little (oh, that's so hard for us moms). To put it succinctly, he said, "Mom, I'm ready. I need to ride the bus." Well, what could she say? The next morning, she walked him to the bus stop and courageously sent him off on his own. One small step for childhood; one giant leap for momkind.

me too, mom

I teach third-grade Sunday school at our church. A few summers ago I attended a Child Evangelism Fellowship crash course in leading a child to Christ. It was an excellent workshop. I took a ton of notes and brought home an entire arsenal devoted to witnessing to children. Oh, I had the best time organizing, highlighting, cataloging, and sifting through all of my newfound treasures of information. Everything was color coordinated and properly filed amongst my other teacher stuff at home. That evening was spent inundating my husband with all the discipleship data I had discovered.

The following day, we attended Sunday service, followed by a birthday celebration for my husband. It was also the night he was to be introduced to our congregation as a newly appointed member of the elder board, following the church potluck we were rushing around getting ready for. Unfortunately, we were running a little behind. The chicken wings were taking too long to simmer in the oven. I could feel the "Great, we're late" anxieties buzzing in my gut. In a move of desperation, I yanked the chicken out of the oven (praying against any and all lingering salmonella cooties) and ordered everyone to the van. We jumped in, sat down, buckled up, and backed out of the garage in record time. It was at this moment that our five-year-old spoke up.

"Mommy, you know how you're always asking me if I want to ask Jesus into my heart?"

Blank look on my face. "Uh, yeah. Why?" I stammered, sneaking a peek at my watch.

"Well, Mom, I want to do it right now," he declared.

"Oh, honey, how about if you do it tonight when we get home and have lots of time to talk about it and snuggle and, well, talk

about it some more, okay?" I prompted.

"No, Mom, I remember you telling me that if I don't have Jesus in my heart, I'll be separated from God forever. I want to be in heaven with Jesus like you and Daddy. Anyway, when you're ready, you're ready, right?"

I looked to my husband, and he summed it up quite well: "He's right. You better do it."

It was an amazing moment there on the grubby floor of our van. We prayed together and went through the steps I had learned the day prior. It was a blessing I will never forget: to be given the privilege of introducing my son to the Savior of his heart. And the emotions I experienced far outweighed any organizational jubilation I had felt the night before. Afterward, I gave him a hug and a kiss. Just as Ben put the van into reverse, Katie piped up: "Me too. I'm ready too!"

You know, as adults some of the biggest decisions in our lives are precluded by an overabundance of thinking, planning, worrying, strategizing, and, above all else, talking. Taken in the right dose, these things are positive elements to include in the decision-making process. Too often, though, they become the vehicles we use for stagnation and indecision. Children, on the other hand, are not worriers. They are really, truly doers. Some of us have more "doer" children than others (I refer you back to the Lego incident). I'm trying to learn from the doers in our household and jump in with childlike enthusiasm when the Lord prompts.

foR such a time as this

One of the doers in Scripture who followed the Lord's prompting was a young Israelite woman by the name of Hadassah, otherwise

known as Esther. As a young girl, Esther was orphaned and left to be raised by her cousin Mordecai. Although Mordecai and Esther were Jews, they lived in Persia as a result of the tribe of Israel being conquered and divided following the reign of King Solomon.

The king at the time was King Xerxes. Queen Vashti and he had somewhat of a falling out, and she was forced to relinquish her crown. So the king did the next logical thing: He ordered a mandatory beauty contest in order to find a new queen. Esther was one of the girls forced into joining this contest. King Xerxes was impressed with the young Hebrew woman, and she became the next queen of Persia.

Following Esther's undesirable queenly promotion, an ugly plot unfolded. The king's assistant, Haman, fashioned a plan to destroy the Jewish people living in Persia. He fooled the king into signing a proclamation of war against all Jews, thereby condemning them to a certain bloody and vicious end. "When Mordecai [Esther's cousin] learned of all that had been done, he tore his clothes, put on sackcloth and ashes, and went out into the city, wailing loudly and bitterly" (Esther 4:1).

Being a queen, Esther was a little removed from the daily news. When she finally heard about Mordecai's actions, she set out to discover the source of his sorrow. She sent for one of the king's attendants and commanded him to go to her cousin to find out what had transpired. The attendant returned with the morbid news of the Jews' inevitable annihilation. He also came bearing the plea from Mordecai for Esther to go before the king in hopes that she could beg for mercy on behalf of the Jews. The key here was this: Xerxes was unaware that Persian Queen Esther was also Jewess Hadassah. Mordecai was a thinker. At the outset of Esther's role as queen, he

had convinced her to keep her nationality a secret, as well as her relationship to him.

Well, Esther was no coward, but she knew that an unsolicited appearance before King Xerxes would more than likely result in her own death. So she quickly reminded Mordecai of that seemingly insignificant detail. His reply to her is this:

> Do not think that because you are in the king's house you alone of all the Jews will escape. For if you remain silent at this time, relief and deliverance for the Jews will arise from another place, but you and your father's family will perish. And who knows but that you have come to royal position for such a time as this? (4:13-14)

I find it interesting that Mordecai provoked her a little bit here. He was her only father figure and had been responsible for her for some time. Translation: He knew all the right buttons to push. "Fine, fine Esther. If you don't want to help out your people, I'm sure someone else will. Someone with the courage to stand up against evil will come forth, and our people will be saved. You and I, however, will be history."

I wonder if Esther was a little bit of a wall climber as a child. She had to have a little vim and vigor in her to become queen of all Persia. Being an orphan, she may have learned the lesson of hard knocks early in life. I think she must have been tougher than she appears at first glance. And I think Mordecai would agree with me. Following his needling note about standing up for the good of her people "for such a time as this," Esther immediately sent a reply to Mordecai:

Go, gather together all the Jews who are in Susa, and fast
for me. Do not eat or drink for three days, night or day. I
and my maids will fast as you do. When this is done, I will
go to the king, even though it is against the law. And if I
perish, I perish. (Esther 4:15-16)

Esther, you go girl! Put in the same situation, I would be so
tempted to form a committee with my maidens in order to rational-
ize, theorize, and strategize the situation to death. Pros and cons
would be charted on the nearest bulletin board. The whole spec-
tacle would closely resemble a scene from *Law and Order*. And
there wouldn't be any of that fasting nonsense. How can one worry
without the wonder of baked goods?

But Esther didn't worry—or strategize, or commiserate on the
phone, or go shop at the local mall. I know, it's difficult to imagine.
Our queen graciously took the prompting of her cousin with diplo-
macy and respect. She faced her adversary and encouraged others
to join her in fasting, which in all likelihood led to some deep soul-
searching prayer to the Lord God of Israel.

And then she did it. She went before the king, knowing she
might die. Esther was a doer, not just a talker. Her example of
righteous, prayer-based action continues to motivate and inspire
believers all over the world. The best part of the story is that she
didn't perish. Haman did, however. Esther bravely approached King
Xerxes and through a dinner-date invitation (we all know the way to
a man's heart) made her people's unavoidable annihilation apparent to him.

The king was outraged at Haman's deceit, and Haman was hung,
Esther was esteemed, her people were protected, and Mordecai was

made manager—he got Haman's old job.

Esther and Mordecai's story is encouraging to over-talkers like me. I need to remember the lessons gleaned from it when I am faced with ugly, vile Hamans of my own. I need to be a doer like Esther and my "anti–Visa ads" climbing up the wall. I want to change the way I address decisions that need to be made. Rather than responding first by picking up the phone, I want to be focused on the Lord as I offer up the petitions of my heart to Him. Instead of fretting myself into ineffective, tormented paralysis, I want to be courageous enough to take that first step, knowing that God will be with me. And if I perish, I perish. Enough of this wondering and worrying for me. Who knows? Perhaps God put me here for such a time as this.

CHAPTER 5

PRAYER RULZ!

A grandfather was walking through his yard when he heard his granddaughter repeating the alphabet in a tone of voice that sounded like a prayer. He asked her what she was doing. The little girl explained: "I'm praying, but I can't think of exactly the right words, so I'm just saying all the letters, and God will put them together for me, because He knows what I'm thinking."

CHARLES B. VAUGHAN

A Chinese proverb says, "A journey of a thousand miles begins with a single step."[8] I would like to borrow and adapt this phrase to say, "The journey of parenting begins with a daily prayer."

In fact, I've noticed that you can classify parental prayers into three primary categories. First, there are Appreciation Prayers. These are where we thank God for the blessings in our lives. I call them warm-fuzzy prayers. Appreciation Prayers typically take place during the hours following bedtime. It's so easy to be thankful when everything is quiet and the kids are sleeping, isn't it? If the house is clean, then it becomes an all-out thanksgiving-fest: "Hallelujah and thank You, Jesus!"

Experience has taught me over the years that motherhood would not be complete without the second type of prayer: Protection Prayers. From the moment we hear that first tiny heartbeat, we embark on a journey fraught with fears, tears, and Protection Prayers. During our first moments of motherhood, our heart becomes fused with that of our child, for better or for worse (for some of us, the fusion takes a little longer!). We pray about diaper rash, ear infections, colic, math tests, recess bullies, stuttering insecurities, teenage acne, driving tests, and future spouses.

But if I included only these two types of prayers, I would be remiss in portraying life as it truly exists (at least in *our* home). While I do hound the throne of heaven with Appreciation Prayers and Protection Prayers on behalf of my children, the types of prayers that get me through every day are Panic Prayers—S.O.S. prayers, you could call them. "Oh, Father God in heaven, sweet Jesus, and Savior of my soul, I need your help, patience, and quick thinking *right now*!"

Panic Prayers don't even have to be lucid. A whimper will get the message across. I have spent a lot of years whimpering to God due to a poor connection between my mental synapses and vocal chords. In pediatric circles they refer to this as "Barney Overdose Effect" (aka B.O.E.). When I discuss this particular medical condition, I receive one of two reactions: (1) grim nods of understanding (these people are in touch with their sharing side), or (2) blank stares. Somehow, there exists in the Western world individuals who have avoided the entire singing-dinosaur phenomenon. This perplexes me. The bummer is that if they've totally missed out on Barney, they will never truly be able to empathize with the rest of us. It's difficult, due to its very nature, to describe the effects of

B.O.E. It must be experienced to be truly appreciated.

I recall a time when my poor synapses were indulged with some empathy from an unlikely source: my brother-in-law Joe. For the record, I must state that Joe is an extremely compassionate and understanding guy. However, he is a guy — a guy, in fact, who is a cardiologist. Am I making myself clear? Dr. Joe spends a large amount of his time working through complex, life-threatening situations from the comfort of his office, with nary a purple dinosaur in sight.

There was a time, however, in the not-too-distant past, when dear Joe spent an entire weekend (approximately forty-two hours) alone with his two toddler-age boys — and Barney. Being a stay-at-home mom suffering the ravages of long-term B.O.E., I was interested to hear Joe's assessment following the conclusion of the Barney-a-thon. This, girlfriends, is a direct quote (I've actually considered custom ordering it for my license plate): "Being a stay-at-home parent is one of the most mind-numbing experiences I have ever encountered."

I cannot express the liberation I experienced following this statement. He understood B.O.E.! He and I and our sad little synapses had bonded. It's a moment I shall always treasure. I have it filed away to relish on another day when my Panic Prayers once again prevail.

tHe fIrst sHaLL Be Last

My husband and I are not the only ones in the family to make use of prayer. Our kids pray too, but this is not necessarily a fact of which I am proud. Evening prayer with our children is probably my least favorite time of the day. I hope the Lord looks past our somewhat

pathetic prayer offerings and straight into our hearts—at least *my* heart. Ben and I spend time with our kids making daily prayer deposits in the bank of parental obedience because we know we should. The unseemly truth is that our children have made a science out of prayer-time argumentation. They categorically fight over:

Who?

> Them: "I don't know who to pray for, Mommy."
> Me: "Why don't you pray for Daddy?"
> Them: "But I don't *wanna* pray for Daddy!"

When?

> "I want to pray before Emma. Emma always gets to pray first!"

Where?

> "Mommy, we're supposed to be at home on the floor next to my own bed when we pray. We can't pray in a tent!"

What?

> Them: "I want to pray for GramPam. What should I pray for?"
> Me: "Why don't you pray that she'll have a good sleep?"
> Them: "No."
> Me: "Okay, why don't you pray that she'll have a safe trip?"
> Them: "No."
> Me: "Good day tomorrow?"
> Them: "Nope. That's not what I'm supposed to pray for. What do you think I should pray for?"

And, of course, **Why?**

> Them: "Why do we pray, Mommy? Why do we fold our
> hands and close our eyes? I don't want to close my
> eyes. Why do we pray at night? I want to pray in the
> morning."

In the midst of the inevitable bedtime turmoil, I tend to use up an entire month's ration of Panic Prayers. It has gotten so bad some evenings that I've barked out, "Sit down and shut up; we're PRAYING!" The term *prayer warriors* has a totally different meaning at the Doucette home. That's not to say the kids haven't come up with some pretty touching prayers, but they seem to be few and far between.

We've had to get creative and establish some basic Prayer Rules of the family. One night our parental wisdom led us to the "eeny, meeny, miney, moe" technique to decide who prayed first. Two-year-old Katie won. Translation: Three-year-old J.J. lost. He glared and fumed as Katie began to pray. She closed her eyes and folded her hands and said in her sweetest voice, "Dear God, thank You that I got to pray FIRST [and here she looked right at J.J.]. Thank you, God, that J.J. will NEVER, EVER, EVER get to pray first, EVER."

It took about a half hour to calm J.J. down. He was in post-traumatic prayer hysterics. It's been several years since then, and we're doing much better. We still occasionally have prayer predicaments.

Unfortunately, our prayer issues are not limited to bedtime. Mealtimes can be challenging as well. One year, rather than fussing over rules at dinner, Ben and I enthusiastically sorted through a list of several traditional mealtime prayers so as to better focus our

evening efforts (okay, and so we could eat sooner). Here is the one we chose: "Thank You, God, this happy day, for food and home and friends and play."

The original plan was to rotate through a series of memorized prayers, but that brought about a new set of problems. Pretty soon they were griping and grappling over which grace to use. Good grief. So we stuck with the "happy day" prayer. We've said it so many times in the last ten years that I'm sure it's permanently imbedded in the fibers of my damaged synapses. I can picture myself in a nursing home years from now, mumbling incoherently to no one in particular about food and home and friends and play. I won't be able to remember my name, but I'm sure I'll still have mealtime prayer down pat.

oN youR maRks, get set, go!

One of the truths about raising children is that it's more like a marathon than a sprint (which is difficult for us sprinter-type people, aka the patience-impaired). Oh, the first few years, there is a lot of growth and change. And then it slows down. The results from time invested in our children's development aren't as tangible as they were during the early years. The baby/toddler stage can be so gratifying for us list makers. Cooing? Check. Smiling? Check. Crawling? Check. Walking? Check. Throwing food on the floor? Check.

For control freaks (uh, that would be me), the early years are more a test of physical caregiving endurance than true parenting. There are all kinds of inventions to assist us in monitoring and controlling the actions of our young children: baby gates, outlet plugs, leashes (which are handy at the mall), car seats, baby moni-

tors, video cameras, and so on. Our prayers tend to run more along the lines of "Please help me get through another day of goldfish crackers, dirty diapers, and Barney."

But as our kids pass those first few childhood milestones, the rest isn't as easy to check off a list. The new list involves matters of the heart: *Is he well-behaved when I'm not around? Does she share? Is he thankful? Is she strong enough to stand up to the bullies at school? Is HE one of the bullies at school?* This is where the marathon aspect of being a mother kicks in.

Unlike when the kids are babies, the rest of parenthood yields few, if any, immediate results. While we can convince ourselves that we are in control of our children when they are babies, it becomes crystal clear as they mature that they are actually under God's jurisdiction. We have to let them go. Thankfully, God gives us the gift of prayer. He allows us the privilege of interceding for them (and the bullies at school). In fact, the most important thing we can do as parents (okay, not counting the food thing) is to daily take our kids before the throne of God.

Getting technical for a moment, *Webster's* defines prayer as "an entreaty; supplication; a humble request, as to God."[9] However, the true characteristic of prayer has nothing to do with being technical! Prayer is emotional, relational, and spiritual. It is crying out to God from the depths of our soul.

I used to buy in to a common misconception about prayer—that prayer changes God. Somehow, like many people, I came to the belief that our prayers can make God change His mind about something, thereby altering His predestined will for our lives. I've since learned it's not so. I know, kind of a bummer. *So what's the point?* I wondered. *What does prayer accomplish?*

Years of crying out to God from the toddler trenches has taught me that when I offer my prayers to Him, I am the one who is changed. If I listen carefully, I hear the heartbeat of God. He gives me perspective and peace in the midst of confused chaos. I learn to trust as I offer my requests to Him, believing that He will bring about the best possible outcome. But it's the best in His ultimate wisdom, not mine! That's where trust comes in.

The Bible is packed with examples of people who have come before God, only to have their prayers answered in unexpected ways. David, Moses, Joseph, Isaiah, Job — the commonality between these men is that their prayers began as Panic Prayers and God tenderly transformed them into Appreciation Prayers. For instance, David, much of whose life was spent escaping from enemies who were bent on killing him, wrote,

On my bed I remember you;
　　I think of you through the watches of the night.
Because you are my help,
　　I sing in the shadow of your wings. (Psalm 63:6-7)

Isaiah, the God-fearing prophet who witnessed the death and spiritual destruction of his people and foretold their inevitable captivity by their enemies, said,

O Lord, you are my God;
　　I will exalt you and praise your name,
for in perfect faithfulness
　　　　you have done marvelous things,
　　　　　　things planned long ago. (Isaiah 25:1)

And dear Job, the man who lost everything and everyone he cherished, humbly said these words to God,

> I know that you can do all things;
>> no plan of yours can be thwarted. . . .
>> Surely I spoke of things I did not understand,
>> things too wonderful for me to know. . . .
> My ears had heard of you
>> but now my eyes have seen you. (Job 42:2-3,5)

It would be easy to read the stories of many great men in the Bible and reach the conclusion that their prayers failed. David's own son turned against him and tried to kill him. Moses died in the wilderness before reaching the Promised Land. Joseph spent years separated from his family, wasting away in a dungeon. Isaiah is said to have been slaughtered by his enemies despite a life spent in sacrificial servitude to God.[10] Their Panic Prayers didn't change God's plans; it was their hearts and attitudes toward Him that were transformed through the journey of faith.

Parenting is no different. Sometimes it feels hopeless to pray for our children's safety on the school bus, until I remember that Jesus Himself prayed for the safety of the children in His life: us. In John 17, Jesus sets a holy example of prayerful petition while staring in the face of His undeserved impending execution. The words He uttered on holy knees are so beautifully pertinent to our children:

> "My prayer is not that you take them out of the world but
> that you protect them from the evil one. They are not of the

world, even as I am not of it. . . . I have made you known to them, and will continue to make you known in order that the love you have for me may be in them and that I myself may be in them." (verses 15-16,26)

It's hard to surrender to the fact that there is real, tangible evil in the world and that we cannot completely protect our children from it. It's so difficult to release them. However, Jesus released His disciples, His "children," the ones dearest to His heart, the ones to whom He had been ministering and teaching. Jesus didn't leave them unequipped, though. He prayed for them—not that they would be "taken out of the world" but that they would be protected by the great I Am.

Every nuance recorded about Jesus in Scripture is a how-to lesson for us. What a comfort to me as a mother. I so yearn to follow His example from John 17:26 of continuing to make God known to my kids so that His love and Spirit will be in them. I have the assurance from the evidence recorded in Scripture that God accepts my Panic Prayers and, through His workmanship, renovates them to Appreciation Prayers—genuine expressions of renewed gratitude.

One morning I was driving our minivan, lamenting our son's behavior. I was turning parental second-guessing into an art form. From the day of his birth, I had harbored the hope that some-day my son would be the next Billy Graham; as I cruised down the highway I was certain that he would most likely grow up to be the next Billy the Kid. Panic Prayers streamed from my sleep-deprived brain as steadily as the tears coursing down my cheeks. Our two young daughters were in the car as I brokenly wept to the Lord. With the innocent bliss of childhood, my girls prattled

in the backseat, unaware of my distress. In the midst of their chattering, our two-year-old started singing the song "God Is So Good." I listened and thanked Him for the reminder. However, He wasn't quite finished. My Katie chorused from the backseat, "Hey, Mommy, I know this song! Let's all sing it together!" And so we sang,

God is so good,
God is so good,
God is so good,
He's so good to me.[11]

One rendition of any song is never enough for my children, so we repeated this verse over and over until my sad little synapses finally giggled and said, "Okay, Lord, I get it!" As I reflected on my two girls and their part in my personal tutorial on trust, I couldn't help but think of the following:

How great is the love the Father has lavished on us, that we should be called children of God! And that is what we are! (1 John 3:1)

Great is the LORD and most worthy of praise; his greatness no one can fathom. (Psalm 145:3)

I had been offering woeful prayers laden with panic and unbelief. In His mercy, He majestically transformed my prayers, like those of David, into Appreciation Prayers.

s.o.s. witHout ceasiNς

The problem with moms and prayer is, of course, the Time Factor. Every one of us struggles to fit prayer into our lives. I used to think there was a special provision in the Bible for moms—you know, an asterisk next to The Lord's Prayer that says, "Except if you're the mother of young children, in which case you're exempt from the requirement to pray."

But I've searched and searched my Bible, and I can't seem to find that verse! So I've come to the unpopular conclusion that, yes, even moms need to find time for prayer. Like I mentioned before, the evening hours after the kids are asleep are a good time for prayer. But if you're like me, sitting or kneeling with head down and eyes closed means sleep! So that leaves the morning time before the kids get up. Unfortunately, I'm not up then, either. What's a mom to do?

This is one of those moments when 1 Thessalonians 5:17 comes in handy. It says, "Pray continually." Remember those S.O.S. prayers we talked about? I don't know about you, but I think they qualify. God wants us to be in constant communication with Him, aware of His continual presence, thanking Him for everything He gives us, praising Him for who He is, and yes, even crying to Him for emergency help. As moms, we can "practice the presence of God" (in the words of Brother Lawrence)[12] as we go through our day by staying in constant communication with Him. I find that the more I do this, the more He miraculously opens up quiet moments in my day or evening when I can sit and truly focus on Him. What a blessing!

I'm certain that prayer time with me is probably no picnic for God. Like my children, I fight and argue over the who/when/

where/what/why of every little thing. The truth is that God is not a patience-impaired, guilt-saddled sprinter who will poop out long before the marathon is over; He is a prayer warrior in the purest sense. Thankfully, with Him there are no prayer rules. The sky's the limit. Go for it, moms: On your marks, get set, go!

CHAPTER 6

NICK @ NITE

*Sometimes I lie awake at night, and I ask, "Where have
I gone wrong?" Then a voice says to me, "This is
going to take more than one night."*

CHARLES M. SCHULTZ

I t's 2:53 a.m. on a Saturday. The kids have long since fallen
asleep after having been read to, snuggled with, prayed over,
and tucked in. You're deep in sleep, trying to catch up on the sleep
you've missed during the last three months. In fact, you're hoping
to sleep in until about noon. Of course, it's only wishful thinking.
Sleeping in until 7:00 a.m. will suffice.

Suddenly, an ear-piercing cry shatters the comfy stillness of the
night. You fumble for your bathrobe and stagger down the hall to
your two-year-old's bedroom. Everything appears to be in order:
nightlight, teddy bear, blanket, toy rocket with the tip chewed off.
All the necessary bedtime paraphernalia seems to be in the correct
location. You tentatively reach over and feel your sobbing little boy's
head, dreading what you will discover. Yep, it's a fever, probably

around 102 or so. With no doctor or appointment in sight for at least fifty-three hours. Drat.

Your rational daytime self says it's only a temporary flu bug, but your nighttime persona immediately drums up its own formidable diagnoses: Massive ear infection? Scarlet fever? What if it's meningitis? You find yourself transforming from the objective, reasonable decision-making Dr. Jekyl to the incoherent, nerve-wracked Ms. Hyde. You know it's too late to legitimately call any of your friends (or even the doctor) for advice, and your husband's snores have moved from light whiffs to freight-train rumbles. The Pediatric Tylenol is merely a crusty purple ring around the bottom of the bottle. The situation becomes all too clear: You and the fever are on your own.

So you go through the middle-of-the-night-fever ritual carried out by mothers all through the ages: rocking, praying, crooning, and worrying the night away while you count down the hours until daylight. Your silent pleas for protection are punctuated by heartfelt thanksgiving to the God of heaven for Winnie the Pooh videos and Nickelodeon. And Jay Jay the Jet Plane. And Raffi. It's going to be a long night.

ςOODNIςHt, sweetHeaRt, ςOODNIςHt

This scene is all too familiar to me, especially with our first child. I remember sleeping on the floor in front of his crib every time he got a cold. I've toughened up a little since then. However, I've never quite recaptured the pre-mommy skill of deep sleeping I once enjoyed. At the first sign of whimpering, coughing, crying, or heavy breathing, I am in my child's doorway, alert and ready to comfort

and problem solve. My children's cries bring me out of bed with catlike reflexes, especially when I have the baby monitor turned up too high. In that case, a loud intake of breath will do it. I usually pay for these nocturnal supervisory sessions the next morning, though. While my husband hops cheerfully out of bed, ready to greet the day, I tend to function at a much groggier, less cheerful level.

The snooze button gets the worst of it: The alarm goes off. I think to myself, *I can shower tomorrow.* Hit the snooze button. Alarm goes off again. *I can drive the kids to school today instead of trying to make it to the bus stop on time.* Snooze button. Alarm once again. *It's been awhile since they bought hot lunch.* Snooze. Alarm. *They can eat breakfast in the car and change out of their jammies in the bathroom during first recess.* Snooze. Snooze. Snooze.

My morning man, on the other hand, is more like a hibernating bear being roused mid-December if somebody wakes him in the middle of the night. His idea of nighttime comforting is to heave himself out of bed and offer helpful advice from the hallway like, "You're okay. G'night."

One night I awoke to the sound of a fever-induced whimper from the crib. I was nursing the other baby and sent Ben to the kitchen with specific instructions: "Bring a cool washcloth, the Pediatric Tylenol, a sippy cup with diluted apple juice, and the nose syringe!"

"I'm all over it," he murmured, and lumbered down the hall roughly in the direction of the kitchen.

I waited several minutes as the sick child's cries turned into shrieks. Several more minutes passed and I started breaking out in a sweat. Finally, Ben emerged in the doorway, looking sheepish.

"Uh, what am I supposed to do again? I can't remember why I was sent to the kitchen, but I was afraid to come back empty-handed."

I can't complain too much. Although Ben takes awhile to wake up, once he's conscious, his support skills kick into high gear. If I get to him before freight-train rumbles, he's more than happy to make an emergency Pediatric Tylenol run to the grocery store.

express yourself

Everything looks different in the middle of the night. I know firsthand that a midnight emergency run to the grocery store for apple juice and cough syrup is nothing like the same trip during the day. It's a particularly memorable event when I get to stand in the express checkout line. Of course, it's usually the only one open at that hour.

Being a type A rule follower, I take great pains to heed the maximum requirement. For some stores it's twelve. Other, more laid-back, chains allow a scandalous fifteen items in their express line. I'm not sure who came up with the "Nine Items or Less" concept, though. This seems a bit harsh. Why not ten? Apparently, grocery stores aren't into rounding their numbers. And does it count to have two or three of the same thing, or is it just nine items, period? These are questions I ponder while waiting in the express checkout.

I'm an adept and highly proficient people watcher. I can't help it—I'm addicted to being nosy! In the attempt to keep my eyes in roam function, I feel my gaze drawn inevitably to the conveyor belt as it lurches toward "my turn." My curiosity is always piqued by choices made by fellow nighttime shoppers. There are the college-aged, lip-locking beer buyers who can barely tear themselves apart to pay for their wares; the rumpled father with whole milk and diapers; the single guy whose culinary taste buds favor frozen dinners. But then

we have the purchases that cry out, "Why have you come out in the middle of the night for . . . [*Cotton balls, sandwich bags, toothpicks, corn starch, gum*]?" Hold it . . . wait a minute . . . that's gum and fast-actin' Tinactin. Aha! It's the old "Add a pack of gum and the significance of my somewhat vulnerable and all-too embarrassing purchase will somehow be diminished" theory: *Maybe they'll think I came to the store for gum and threw in the foot fungus cream as an afterthought.* We've all done it.

I GO OUT WALKIN' AFTER MIDNIGHT

Emergency runs to the grocery store, late-night trips to the ER, 2 a.m. feedings, toddler night terrors, and the times we mothers can't sleep because we're worrying about our children and overanalyzing our parenting skills. Doesn't it seem that everything is intensified at night?

I'm thinking there's a reason for our heightened nocturnal neuroses. Is it possible that God can use the nighttime worrying and wondering to bring us closer to Himself? Let's take a look at someone else who was worrying at night—and decided to find some answers for his questions.

> Now there was a man of the Pharisees named Nicodemus,
> a member of the Jewish ruling council. He came to Jesus
> *at night* and said, "Rabbi, we know you are a teacher
> who has come from God. For no one could perform the
> miraculous signs you are doing if God were not with him."
> (John 3:1-2, emphasis added)

I'm not sure why Nicodemus approached Jesus at night. As a prestigious member of the Jewish high council, the Sanhedrin, he would have had access to Jesus anytime he wished. But Nicodemus was a Pharisee, and Jesus was unimpressed with the Pharisees. He saw through their righteous acts, straight into their hearts. His words to the Pharisees are recorded several times in the book of Matthew:

> "Woe to you, teachers of the law and Pharisees, you
> hypocrites! You shut the kingdom of heaven in men's
> faces. You yourselves do not enter, nor will you let those
> enter who are trying to." (Matthew 23:13)

> "Woe to you, teachers of the law and Pharisees, you
> hypocrites! You clean the outside of the cup and dish,
> but inside they are full of greed and self-indulgence."
> (Matthew 23:25)

> "Woe to you . . . Pharisees. . . . You are like whitewashed
> tombs, which look beautiful on the outside but on the
> inside are full of dead men's bones and everything
> unclean." (Matthew 23:27)

Woe! Woe! Whoa! Nicodemus had some fairly significant worries on his mind. Hypocrites? Never get into heaven? It's no wonder he sneaked out in the safety of the evening shadows to meet with the Rabbi, the man named Jesus, who spoke with such authority. Nicodemus was compelled to bring his worries, concerns, and questions to Jesus in search of the answers he was supposed to have already known.

In reply Jesus declared, "I tell you the truth, no one can see the kingdom of God unless he is born again."

"How can a man be born when he is old?" Nicodemus asked. "Surely he cannot enter a second time into his mother's womb to be born!"

Jesus answered, "I tell you the truth, no one can enter the kingdom of God unless he is born of water and the Spirit. Flesh gives birth to flesh, but the Spirit gives birth to spirit. . . . For God so loved the world that he gave his one and only Son, that whoever believes in him shall not perish but have eternal life. For God did not send his Son into the world to condemn the world, but to save the world through him." (John 3:3-6,16-17)

Jesus knew Nick's heart and his internal struggles. He patiently listened, comforted, and imparted truth and the message of salvation under the peaceful cover of darkness.

Nicodemus was brave. His fellow Pharisees would have certainly gotten their tassels in a twist had they known of his clandestine meeting with Jesus. The Lord's words clearly hit the mark, though. Nicodemus became a new man. His insomnia had provided an opportunity to meet with the Lord in private. He was able to bring his questions and misunderstandings without any distractions, and his life was changed because of it.

Is it possible that we too can use those nighttime worries, frustrations, and confusions for good? Will He listen to us? Will He answer us? Nicodemus set such a good example. He went right to the Source of all truth. And the Source of all truth listened and answered.

Our woes will never fully disappear. However, we can find comfort in the One who offers us spiritual rebirth and eternal life. The next time you find yourself alone and awake in the middle of the night, remember Nicodemus. Rather than allowing yourself to become overwhelmed by your woes, bring them to the Lord in the peacefulness of moonlight. You won't even be limited to the express lane—He can handle a passel of woes.

We, like Nicodemus, might not fully understand His answers. But once we bring our questions out of the darkness to Him, He promises to transform them into light.

foibles and fowl-ups

*Physically there is nothing to distinguish human society from
the farm-yard except that children are more troublesome and
costly than chickens and calves and that men and women
are not so completely enslaved as farm stock.*

GEORGE BERNARD SHAW

"We're going to have to kill the rooster." These ominous
words from my husband, Ben, flew across the room
and wrapped themselves around my groggy morning head.

"Huh?" I moaned.

"He's making too much noise; we're going to tick off the neighbors. We need to get rid of him."

Get rid of him? Easy for *him* to say. Katie, our six-year-old, had
already shed buckets of tears when informed that we were probably
going to give him away to a loving family. (Where we were going to
find a loving rooster family was beyond me.) *Wait till she finds out
Daddy wants to kill him*, I thought. He had originally entertained
thoughts of serving the cock-a-doodler on a plate with mashed
potatoes and gravy, but it quickly became clear that for our family,

a slaughtered pet does not a dinner make. And we actually never meant to get a rooster in the first place.

It all began with a teachers' strike. It was September, the month all moms look forward to after a long hot summer. Suddenly, we were faced with no school! As a stress reliever and boredom buster, we decided to try our hands at being chicken farmers. In between rallies and protest marches, we built our own chicken coop. Ben and the kids drove to a friend's house and arrived home hours later with four grown chickens. About a week later, they proudly displayed four baby chicks they obtained from the local co-op. Farmer Ben and his cohorts threatened to bring home still more, but I finally put my foot down. (Those little things poop a ton.)

You know, it's always interesting to hear someone else's take on a decision like becoming chicken owners. My mother, in fact, claims I am the absolute last person in our family she thought would be a chicken farmer. I didn't ask her why. (Apparently, everyone else is more fowl-minded than I am.) Perhaps it's the whole germaphobic thing coming back to haunt me. Be that as it may, we are chicken farmers and loving every minute of it. We've actually added three more babies to the mix; unfortunately, one of them ended up being a rooster. With chickens, you never know the gender until he breaks forth with his first prepubescent rooster call. As of today, his fate is still on the line. I'll keep you posted.

the trouble with fish

Strangely enough, right about the time the poultry urges hit, Ben and I also felt the need to be fish owners. Call it early "empty nest" syndrome. My husband is adamantly opposed to pets with fur,

teeth, and verbal articulation (the poor rooster), so the kids and I have had to get a little creative in order to appease our deep-seated pet-owner urges. Between chicken coop remodels and hourly egg hunting, we made numerous trips to the local pet store in search of fish food, vitamins, and the necessary tank flora.

Fish are great pets. They're fairly clean and quiet and don't scratch up the furniture. They are so peaceful to watch as they weave in and out of the water staring up at our grotesquely distorted faces peering in at them.

However, the trouble with fish is that they are difficult to keep alive. Right about the time we'd get all the kinks worked out, we'd find the fish on its side. It's tough to form a bond with a creature that only lives in your house for a grand total of five days. Over the course of about two months, we held so many graveside services in the backyard that I eventually lost count. I'm not sure the pet-store owner will even sell us another fish. Truth be told, we inevitably lost interest in our fine-finned friends. I guess you can't mix your agricultural and aquatic skills. No more water pets for us. We've got a great stash of fish food, though, if you're interested.

so, Do you feeL Lucky?

Because there are no dogs in our pet-owning future (dogs have fur, teeth, and verbal articulation), I've decided to live my canine ownership vicariously through my two younger sisters. One sister owns a chocolate lab called Riley, and the other has a golden retriever named Rufus (names have been changed to protect the innocent, thereby removing any possible hurt doggy-niece feelings).

I'm sorry to say that Riley is a jumper and a sniffer. (You know what

I mean.) Maybe you have experienced this scenario. You innocently drive up to someone's house and get out of the car. A large wet dog comes bounding out of nowhere, full speed ahead. Before you can get a word out of your mouth, the wet dog has wedged herself between you and your car and has begun the sniffing process in the absolute last place you want that wet dirty nose to be: right in your, well, um, you know. You chuckle nervously and push the dog away. This only aggravates the sniffing. The more forceful you get, the more frenzied the sniffing becomes. Finally, the dog owner comes out of the house in a huff, all the while scolding the offending pup, who looks at you with soulful eyes and a look that says, "Gee, I was just being friendly."

Rufus, though, is my kind of dog. She is so sweet. She's got a facial expression straight out of *Where the Red Fern Grows*. I swear she knows what I'm thinking sometimes. She spends her time snuggling on the porch with her two kittens and trying to finagle an opportunity to fetch for anyone who walks by. Her tail is in perpetual wag-motion. She neither jumps nor sniffs. Okay, strictly between you and me, she's my favorite doggy-niece. Unfortunately, when you are in the business of purchasing an adorable puppy, they are not marked "jumper and sniffer" versus "tail-wagging sweetie pie." They all look basically the same. When you decide to become a dog owner you put the future of your yard, as well as all your friends' clean clothing, on the line. When in the market for a good dog, you simply must ask yourself, *Do I feel lucky?*

sepaRatiNg tHe sHeep fRom tHe goats

A friend of mine grew up on a small farm complete with chickens, dogs, and cats, with a few geese thrown in for good measure.

One afternoon my friend's dad came home with the idea to put more lactose into their life. They soon became goat owners as well. Naphtali, as the new little goat soon became called, rose to Favored Pet status in spite of her deficient milk production. Their sweet little goat was taught to kiss and would even jump up to rub noses, to the delight of the children in the household. Dad was not so amused with these antics and decided after two years of unsuccessful breeding to put her to better use. Poor Naphtali was sentenced to the butcher block. However, in honor of their high regard for their beloved pet, the children declared they would never eat poor Naphtali. A few months later, after a wonderful spaghetti dinner, the youngsters were asked if they had enjoyed their dinner. My unsuspecting friend and her siblings unanimously praised the spaghetti dinner, claiming it the best they'd ever had. Their dad looked at them and quipped, "Must have been the meeeaaat."

Family pets. They range from puppies to guppies. Parents typically have a love/hate relationship with the family pets. While giving us an outlet for affection and comic relief, they also provide an opportunity for some important life lessons: hygiene, reproduction, birth, and death. In the Bible, God also uses images from the animal kingdom to teach us important life lessons. He is the Keeper of the sheep:

> Know that the LORD is God.
>> It is he who made us, and we are his;
>> we are his people, the sheep of his pasture. (Psalm 100:3)

In John 10, Jesus refers to Himself as the shepherd caring for His flock: "I am the good shepherd. The good shepherd lays down

his life for the sheep. . . . I am the good shepherd; I know my sheep and my sheep know me" (verses 11,14).

I don't know much about sheep. The one thing I do know is that they are half a fish short of a full tank, if you get my meaning. Apparently, they are such simplistic beasts that mere children were given the task of caring for them in ancient days. The shepherds were young boys and girls from the local village. These youngsters followed the sheep all day; they used only their voices to direct the sheep to protected areas of food and water.

As the children spoke to their herd, the sheep grew so accustomed to the sound of their own particular shepherd that they would follow no other. In fact, the trust between sheep and shepherd was such that "a simple call from their shepherd was sufficient for an entire flock to follow his lead."[13]

This is an important key in protecting the sheep from the long line of sheep-eating predators. In real life, Wylie E. Coyote is one dangerous dude. I learned a new word in my researching: predation. It means "the act of predators killing sheep." Evidently, predation accounts for almost half of all sheep deaths in the world, resulting in the single largest cause of all sheep mortality.[14]

Sheep need to be protected not only from predators but also from their own poor choices in life. (Sound familiar?) They tend to be big-time overeaters. They have no self-control. In addition, their defense mechanism in a dangerous situation is to flee instead of stay and fight. I don't know if you've ever seen a sheep run before; I would hardly describe it as "making time." In a sentence, they're slow, dumb, cowardly overindulgers. (I refer to the Scripture verses in which the Bible describes *us* as being *sheep*.)

So what about the shepherd? A shepherd must be diligent

because of the many dangers lurking in wait for the sheep. Without a shepherd, the entire herd would be in danger of starvation. It is his responsibility to direct the sheep to green pastures and a safe water source. Diligent, responsible, dependable, trustworthy—these words describe Jesus, our Good Shepherd.

Understandably, we mothers tend to see ourselves as the shepherd rather than as sheep. We see the evil that lurks in the world, and our "good mom" instincts want to protect the little sheep entrusted to our care. We often fail to remember that we have a Real Shepherd, the Good Shepherd, who desires to provide for our needs, protect us from harm, and satisfy our deepest longings.

Jesus said,

"My sheep listen to my voice; I know them, and they follow me. I give them eternal life, and they shall never perish; no one can snatch them out of my hand. My Father, who has given them to me, is greater than all; no one can snatch them out of my Father's hand." (John 10:27-29)

These words are such a relief to my simplistic sheep mind. While my strength is so inadequate, it is immensely comforting to realize that no one can snatch us out of God's hand—no one. He is the ultimate Predation Protector.

Having thus come to grips with my spiritually simpleminded sheep status, I have an announcement to make to all of you moms out there:

Dear fellow sheep. Or is it sheeps? No, it's sheep. Dear fellow sheep: Apparently the Wolf we've been trying to

evade for years now is very much alive and well. While
at times it may be exhilarating to attempt escape on
our own, be it through food or flight, we must concede
the inadequacies of all former attempts. Face it: We are
slow, dumb overindulgers. The Good Shepherd knows
this about us and loves us unconditionally in spite of it.
I strongly entreat you to join me in following the Good
Shepherd. We sheep must stick together. That is pretty
much the one thing we do well. The Good Shepherd's
references are impeccable, as is His reputation. The Wolf
has never, I repeat *never*, been able to snatch one of the
Good Shepherd's flock away from Him. While this alone
seals His position as Good Shepherd, I have one final item
to disclose: Our particular Shepherd has actually put His
own life on the line in defense of our eternal safety. At this
moment, death holds no sting for this dear Shepherd. Let's
give Him our allegiance, for without Him, our lives would
be exceedingly and irrevocably baaaad.

May the God of peace, who through the blood of the
eternal covenant brought back from the dead our Lord
Jesus, that great Shepherd of the sheep, equip you with
everything good for doing his will, and may he work in us
what is pleasing to him, through Jesus Christ, to whom be
glory for ever and ever. Amen. (Hebrews 13:20-21)

chapter 8

NO PAIN, NO GAIN

*Giving birth is like taking your lower lip and
forcing it over your head.*

Carol Burnett

For the stork's delivery of our first child, my husband and I decided to fly solo (well, besides the doctor, of course). We anticipated a time of bonding between us, unmarred by the presence of others. To be honest, I didn't know how I'd do in the whole transitional labor thing. I wanted as few spectators as possible in case my pain threshold took a major nosedive.

Before you get the idea that swarms of individuals were lined up outside Room 316, it was my mother, my father, and my sister. My mother, in particular, was extremely put out that she couldn't be in the room. We were unyielding, however. So while I panted and moaned, my hungry and bored husband munched on dough-nuts and read the paper. While I tried to get my breathing in the right rhythm, he put his coffee-scented face too close to mine and exhaled at all the wrong times. When my back hurt, he massaged

too hard; when I wanted the nurse, he tried to talk me out of it. "She's probably busy," he said. "I'm sure you're going to be fine."

Never in my life had I appreciated my mother's sacrifices as much as when I gave birth. I couldn't believe she had gone through this experience for me! Stabs of guilt prickled my conscience as my feisty teenage years flashed through my mind. What was I thinking to treat her like that?

With the final push to introduce our son into the world, the enormous significance of Mother's Day struck. Suddenly, all those azalea plants my sisters and I had carelessly presented to my mom every May seemed shamefully inadequate. This woman had given birth three times! She had rightfully earned an annual endowment of a Japanese maple—well, an oak tree at least. The point is, our mom should have had an entire grove of towering foliage to her credit. I reached an important conclusion in the labor and delivery wing in 1995: No more cheap shrubs for Mother's Day.

And while the birth was a miraculous ordeal that indeed brought Ben and me closer, for the second child, I had one change to make: I wanted my mommy, because during the laborious act of giving birth, I wanted someone with a little more experience.

So for delivery number two, my mom and Ben were both present. It was a much better arrangement. She was the buffer between me and coffee breath, as well as my "Get the nurse" advocate. None of this "She's probably busy" nonsense. The only glitch in the plan was that my mother had met the doctor before. At his own house. At a barbecue. She hadn't realized it, though, until the stitching-up process had begun.

As I grimaced and groaned through the ordeal, she and he compared notes and found that indeed they had met one another in the

nonmedical world. After a few minutes of friendly banter, I had had enough. "Hey, you two are not supposed to know each other outside of the medical world. This is not the time to be talking about decking material and gardening tips. You are a doctor who lives at the hospital, who I will never have the opportunity to see in a social setting. Are we clear here?" Soon after, my medication kicked in and they were free to discuss the wonders of Miracle-Gro.

For our third child, I happily sent Ben, his newspaper, and his coffee to wait in the hallway until the last possible minute. "Are you sure this is okay?" he asked tentatively in the doorway. "This isn't one of those times when you say one thing and then you're going to hold it against me for the rest of my life?" Silly man. I wanted him outta there. "No, dear. You're no good to me afterward if you use up your energy too early. You need to pace yourself." He gleefully took his place in the waiting room, like so many fortunate fathers from the previous generation.

REFERRED PAIN

I learned a term in college called *referred pain*. It is "pain that is felt at a place in the body different from the injured or diseased part where the pain would be expected."[15] Anyone who's ever drunk a milkshake too fast and gotten "brain freeze" is familiar with referred pain. We can't feel pain in our esophagus, the body part that's actually being injured, so the body sends the pain to that spot between our eyes where we *can* feel it. Moms, for the most part, are the primary pain takers of the family. In the familial body, the appendage known as "the mother" accrues a hefty amount of referred pain throughout her lifetime. At our house, we call it

"takin' it for the team." The pain of motherhood is in no way limited to the delivery room. It starts in infancy and extends throughout our children's adulthood, till death do us part:

- Crawling on the floor in the middle of the night looking for the pacifier: takin' it for the team.
- Enduring a barrage of head-butts to the upper lip during the fussy toddler stage: takin' it for the team.
- Running barefoot to the bus stop in your jammies to get the kids on the bus on time: takin' it for the team.
- Hosting a slumber party for a group of giggling ten-year-old girls: big-time takin' it for the team.

Our pain threshold definitely inches up a few notches when we become mothers. We're tough chicks. Strangely enough, no one has yet to fashion a mom superhero to counteract Spidey and Superman. Can you picture it?

Faster than a speeding toddler, more powerful than a
    loaded diaper,
Able to leap in front of oncoming cars in a single bound.
Look! Up in the Sky! It's a bird, it's a plane . . .
It's SuperMom!

Yes, it's SuperMom, strange visitor from another planet who came to earth with powers and abilities far beyond those of mortal men. SuperMom, who can change the course of mighty teenagers; take care of bloody noses, barf, and bowel movements with her bare hands; and who, disguised as an overworked homemaker, fights the

never-ending battle for truth, justice, and her own way.

Sigh. I could use a superhero like that. Sheesh, I could use a spandex suit like that. My pain threshold may be higher, but my daily exercise limit is much lower. Three rounds of pregnancy, potty training with M&M's, and the excess amount of time sitting in my van shuttling others to afterschool practice has wreaked some serious havoc with my pre-baby bod. I'm sporting the same mom-physique I once naively vowed never to possess. When Victoria's Secret accidentally sends me a catalogue, I just laugh. And then I cry, because I have yet to discover her secret—although I bet it includes a potpourri of liposuction, tummy tucks, botox, and breast augmentation.

My own secret is that I would love to look as good on the out-side as Sophia Loren at age seventy; however, in my heart, I know I would rather be like the Velveteen Rabbit, worn-out but well loved.

GROWING PAINS

We named one of our daughters after my best friend from junior high, Katie Baldwin. From grades seven to eleven, I spent a lot of time at Katie's house, which was just around the corner, through the neighbor's backyard. While my own family's oddities annoyed me, the Baldwin family quirks were both endearing and entertaining. I have fond memories of watching her dad create a painting, of listening to her brother regale us with his skiing adventures (and his alleged girlfriend adventures), of teasing her sisters, and of talking with her mother.

Katie's mom, Helen, possessed the ability to maintain chaos with gentleness and graciousness. Among other things, she spent

her time mowing the lawn, sewing ballet costumes, hauling kids to piano lessons in their big old blue suburban, and listening to the adolescent ramblings of her children's friends. She and I spent a lot of time chatting over grilled cheese sandwiches and Tang. A multi-talented homemaker, she was a woman I deeply admired.

One day I asked Katie about the ever-present Ace bandage around Helen's left arm. Her answer was the last thing I expected: "She's in remission from breast cancer." I couldn't believe it. She seemed so healthy, so vibrant, so alive, and so at peace.

After recovering from the initial surprise of Helen's health situation, I succumbed to the complacency common to a self-absorbed teenager. Katie and I graduated, and we all went our separate ways. A year later I received news that Helen had died from breast cancer. I was devastated, and I determined to attend her funeral. At her memorial service, there was a modest display set up to honor her life. On a table toward the front of the sanctuary was a picture of Helen, and next to it, her Bible. I have yet to see another Bible in such a sorry condition. To say that it was well used is an understatement. The thing was trashed. The leather cover was faded and discolored, the edges bent completely over the binding. The pages were creased and folded from a lifetime of use. Helen had accomplished a difficult feat: She had worn out a Bible.

And yet it was the most beautiful Bible I had ever seen. Helen had invested hours poring over the words of God. Her strength, graciousness, gentleness, and wisdom took on new significance because I saw them as reflections from her heavenly Father. She hadn't kept the Scriptures at a distance, content to showcase them in pristine condition. She read them, absorbed them, used them, taught them, and lived them.

Helen's Bible was also a reflection of her life. Bruised and worn-out, she lived her life to serve and teach others. Her cover may have been a little faded, but her pages of wisdom were eagerly thumbed through time and time again. She was a woman who had undergone the painful process of becoming Real.

Whenever I worry about the pain I have faced or will face as a mother, I think of Helen's Bible and the godly example she still is for me. I can't imagine the pain she must have felt when she said goodbye to her husband and children. It hurts to let someone you love go. It hurts to grow. It hurts to become Real. It hurts to be a mom.

the problem of pain

George MacDonald once wrote, "The Son of God suffered unto the death, not that men might not suffer, but that their sufferings might be like His."[16] Whether you gave birth to your child with an epidural or without, whether you adopted a child or gained a child through marriage, the common denominator of all moms is pain—lots of it. Physical, social, spiritual, emotional, even mental. In fact, parenting can be described as one long succession of painful experiences—from labor to summer slivers to teaching them how to ride a bike to their first heartbreak to dropping them off at college.

Of course, our children have their own pain. How do they handle it? They come to us. They trust our love and our capacity to ease their sufferings. We—who are mortal, vulnerable, and severely limited in our abilities—are the go-to guys in our kiddos' times of need. Who do *we* go to? My dear friend Helen went to her Bible. Her pain was real, yet the gain she received from the words

of God was apparent to anyone who met her.

The pain of parenting is often surprising, but God shows us through pain how to live victoriously and how to rely on Him. He is our seasoned Savior. The sufferings He experienced on the cross of Calvary far surpass our own meager trials. When we bring our pain to Him, He doesn't minimize it. Like a loving father, He lifts us to Himself and comforts us.

Let's toddle in our children's footsteps; let's run to Him unashamedly and tell Him the depths of our hurt. Be encouraged! "What can be seen is temporary, but what cannot be seen is eternal" (2 Corinthians 4:18). Only God can understand our pain. He is our Divine Doula. We need to remember to breathe deeply and stay focused on Him.

Remember the old saying "No pain, no gain"? Them's fightin' words, my friend. If I have to endure suffering to experience spiritual Realness and leave a legacy of love and sacrifice, then bring it on. When it's my turn for a display to honor my life, I want it to include a ratty, well-worn Bible. I want my family to remember my laugh lines and stretch marks, the sacrifices made to bring them into the world. I want them to know I loved them more than myself and that I had no regrets.

CHAPTER 9

WHO'S ON first?

If a woman has to choose between catching a fly ball and saving
an infant's life, she will choose to save the infant's life without
even considering if there is a man on base.

DAVE BARRY

You realize, of course, that it's all about the snack. It's not the cool uniform, leather glove, real cleats, or even winning. It's what the "mom of the day" brought for the kids to eat after the game. How do I know this? Because it's the main topic of conversation in our home until the next game. And while my son cares neither where I sit during the game nor how much of the game I can rehash with him afterward, he has explicit directions and requests regarding the snack I am to provide on my most honored of game days. I'm told that at some point between the elementary years and full-blown puberty, this does change and winning the game becomes the primary focus. But for those first few years, the snack's the thing.

Talk about pressure! While I know that the Red Sox would opt for chips, pop, and candy, I am more inclined to slip them all carrot

sticks, bottled water, and a crunchy red delicious. This, I've learned, is a fate worse than being skunked by the last-place team in the league. Compromise is the name of our game. I usually concede to chips and Gatorade and then toss in an apple to help ease my mom-conscience.

a League of tHeir own

Little League cracks me up—especially T-ball. These little guys take teamwork to a whole new level. T-ball is the only game in which you see the left fielder, pitcher, and catcher running after the same ball. I actually watched a batter fight off the opposing team to field the ball he just hit!

I played as a six-year-old, so I know how boring it can be for a right fielder; even though the ball is stationary on the T, it takes a lot of swings for the batter to actually make contact. Because most batted balls land within close proximity of the hitter, an outfielder has little or no chance of seeing, let alone touching, the ball. Pee Wee outfielders find ways to amuse themselves, though. They spend their time lying in the grass looking for bugs, picking their noses, spinning around in circles, waving to the crowd, building sand castles in the dirt, or crying. There's usually one kid per team who tracks the game and knows what's going on.

On my son's first day of Little League, we showed up for practice and he ran out to the pitcher's mound to join eight of his new teammates. I glanced away for a couple of minutes to search for familiar faces in the crowd of parents. When I looked back, I did a double take: All nine of the boys were pointing at their crotches and proudly pounding on their brand new athletic cups. "Look!" I heard

one declare, "It doesn't even hurt!" Shortly thereafter, they all threw themselves to the ground and began thrashing around in the mud in a very good group simulation of the "Stop, drop, and roll" drill. Oh my, they were having a blast. I glanced at another mother. We rolled our eyes and mentally tallied the extra loads of laundry we would be doing for the next ten years.

What I don't understand about Little League are the irate fathers who pace up and down the baseline screaming at the little guys to get their act together. Their act together? Are they kidding? As mothers, we know that six- and seven-year-olds still occasionally battle with bed-wetting, nightmares, shoe tying, and car rides longer than eight and a half minutes. Each Little Leaguer represents a mother who has done the miraculous: located, washed, and assembled the entire baseball uniform, down to the glove. Gosh, in my mind, if a baseball player shows up on time fully clothed and stands on the field, his act is most definitely together. Any level of athletic contribution to the game is a bonus.

fieLd of Dreams

Having grown up watching my dad play summer softball, I am no stranger to the many nuances of baseball. I proudly held the title of "batgirl" for many seasons. My first crush was at the tender age of thirteen on a twenty-three-year-old shortstop on my dad's team. When you're a thirteen-year-old batgirl, there's something so cool about a guy who can hit a ball, catch a ball, throw a ball, and, well, spit. I've since refined my standards for the ideal man. My husband, however, can spit with the best of them.

Although I was a dandy bat girl, I struggled with the basics of

baseball. In short, I couldn't hit, throw, or catch all that well. Other than that, I was pretty good, except that I was a slow runner. My two sisters, however, were made for softball. Tiffany was a center fielder and Kim a second baseman. And because my dad had played for so many years, I figured it was something I needed to do. In fact, as a baseball family, one of our favorite tunes was one sung by Peter, Paul, and Mary called "Right Field":

Saturday summers, when I was a kid
We'd run to the schoolyard and here's what we did
We'd pick out the captains and we'd choose up the teams
It was always a measure of my self-esteem
Cuz the fastest, the strongest, played shortstop and first
The last ones they picked were the worst
I never needed to ask, it was sealed.
I just took up my place in right field.
Playing right field, it's easy, you know.
You can be awkward and you can be slow.
That's why I'm here in right field just watching the dandelions
    grow.[17]

We belted this little ditty at the top of our lungs from the back-seat of our wood-paneled station wagon for years. Although it was never verbally expressed, I knew in my heart that the song was dedicated to me, the baseball spaz of the family.

Nevertheless, as a teenager I was determined to showcase my latent baseball talent; I decided to try out for the high school girls' junior varsity softball team, along with my freshman sister, who had an incredibly strong throwing arm. (Somehow I never saw *that* red

flag.) Of the thirty-seven players who turned out for the team, I was one of two cut from the team. The other was a sweet girl who suffered with arthritis. She ended up being the manager of the team. As much as it pains me to say it, even though it was only high school junior varsity, I was still way out of my league.

When the actual moment of being "cut" occurred, I was sorely disappointed as well as humiliated. However, I was also surprisingly relieved. I had rallied, failed, and survived. Accepting my demotion from fielder to fan, I moved on to something better-suited: politics. I ran for senior class treasurer/secretary and hung up my baseball dreams and hand-me-down cleats forever. I don't mind telling you, though, I would have made one heck of an umpire.

talkin' baseball

I've often mused over the universal fascination with baseball. Why do we love it so much? How did it earn the title "America's Favorite Pastime"? In part, I think we are enamored with the game because it encompasses so much of everyday life in nine innings and a seventh-inning stretch:

- It's about being vulnerable and trying new things.
- It's about putting on the right equipment for protection against the Enemy's hits.
- It's about working together as a team toward a common goal.
- It's about trusting the base coach to get you home safely.
- It's learning to win—and to lose.
- It's stepping up to the plate and taking your best shot.

Baseball is a lot like motherhood, isn't it?

As for being a mom, I know I'm not the only fair-weather fan out there. The sunny seasons of peace and quiet absolutely launch me out of my seat with a cheer. The torrential downpour of tears and trials, however, cause me to rethink my entire game plan. On most days I feel more like the rookie of the team trying to keep up with the pros. My stats are not pretty; right now, my discipline strategies are in a slump, my batting average is the pits, and my errors outnumber my home runs.

When we all go on a road trip, the kids definitely have the home-field advantage. Any attempt by the pitcher (me) to intimidate the batter (them) is eventually recognized as a balk, and they advance to first base. Right at the moment I attempt to execute a bluff, they distract me with a steal, accomplish an illegal play behind my back, and thereby delay the game until the dust settles.

The clearest example I can provide for this scenario is any trip to the grocery store in which the children outnumber the adults. Their offense strategy is both ingenious and simple: whine and distract. While kid number one gripes his way through each aisle, kids number two and three quickly stock the cart with merchandise preferable to broccoli and deodorant. They know our threats are merely attempts to maintain control. The whole situation is a classic example of what parental peer pressure does to us. While we cringe at the whine-fest displayed by our children, society has certainly put a chokehold on any type of punitive action, so we resort to the method we most abhorred before we became parents: bribery. "Okay, guys, here's the deal. If you don't scream, whine, beg, cry, fight, or freak out from now until we get to the bakery, you can have a chocolate chip cookie. And then if the good behavior continues,

you can get a sticker at the checkout. But only if you're *really* good. I mean it." Oh dear, how far we have fallen. You know you're fighting a losing battle when you use the pathetic words "I mean it."

As mothers in the baseball season of life, we're sometimes able to rally and pull off the old double switch while calling in the closing pitcher: Daddy. While I fancy myself a power pitcher (though I throw more wild pitches than I care to admit), Ben is our finesse pitcher. He is more interested in the control aspect of the game. Able to hold his own each inning, he is undaunted by the kids' attempts to steal and is able to pick them off one by one. His curveball skills have earned him my vote for the Most Valuable Player for nine years running.

Like many couples, our parenting skills tend to be very different from one another. Each of us possesses a strength that counters the other's weakness. My weakness is that my fuse is a little too short and my gunpowder a little too concentrated. Ben's fuse is a bit too long and his gunpowder nonexistent. We are two different coaches running the same baseball clubhouse. When my verbal communication skills are reduced to threats and snarls, he is able to enter the foray with a healthy contribution like, "Okay, now let's talk about the situation calmly and resolve our differences." While I can in no way relate to this strategy, I have seen its success over the years. The man has earned my trust. No baseball game would be complete without a little emotion, so he keeps me around for comic relief.

angels in the outfield

I'm a Seattle Mariners fan until the bitter end, and this season, it looks like that's exactly what kind of end it's going to be. Right now

we have nine wins and sixteen losses. The season's just getting started, though. Slumps come and go, and we're due for a victory. The only thing that will truly kill us is if we sustain more injuries. Our opponents' greatest advantage is targeting our weaknesses and countering with a formidable offensive strategy.

The two fundamental strategies to baseball are maintaining a healthy body and protecting it with the right equipment. You may know where I'm going with this. In Ephesians 6:10-12, Paul wrote these words of encouragement:

Finally, be strong in the Lord and in his mighty power.
Put on the full armor of God so that you can take your
stand against the devil's schemes. For our struggle is not
against flesh and blood, but against the rulers, against
the authorities, against the powers of this dark world and
against the spiritual forces of evil in the heavenly realms.

"Spiritual forces of evil." Sounds a little like something from a 1950s horror movie! So let's get back to baseball—it's a little friendlier. For the sake of demonstration, we'll look at two teams. The Mariners will be us, the strong in the Lord, and the spiritual forces of evil will be, oh, say the New York Yankees.

The two most foolish moves we can make are underestimating our rival's strengths and downplaying our own weaknesses. The Yankees would like nothing better than for us to get overconfident and drop our guard. Imagine an arrogant batter saying something like, "Oh, I don't believe that the Yankee pitcher exists, and even if he did, he couldn't hurt me. Batting helmet? Who needs it?" Odds are, our cocky player would get beaned in

the head with the first pitch.

Spiritual forces do exist. There are both angels and demons in the outfield. Satan's game plan is to entice us to let down our guard so that we enter onto the playing field ill-equipped to do battle. But what is the right equipment? Thankfully, Paul continues with a specific inventory in Ephesians:

> Therefore put on the full armor of God, so that when the
> day of evil comes, you may be able to stand your ground,
> and after you have done everything, to stand. Stand firm
> then, with the belt of truth buckled around your waist,
> with the breastplate of righteousness in place, and with
> your feet fitted with the readiness that comes from the
> gospel of peace. In addition to all this, take up the shield
> of faith, with which you can extinguish all the flaming
> arrows of the evil one. Take the helmet of salvation and
> the sword of the Spirit, which is the word of God. And
> pray in the Spirit on all occasions with all kinds of prayers
> and requests. With this in mind, be alert and always keep
> on praying for all the saints. (6:13-18)

Our armor-clad individual reminds me of a properly outfitted baseball catcher, whose uniform consists of the following equipment:[18]

1. Athletic Supporter. This is an undergarment worn to hold the protective cup in place which defends the, uh, vulnerable parts of the player. The athletic supporter (okay, stick with me here) is kind of like the belt of truth. Without protection against falsehood, the entire foundation crumbles.

2. Chest Protector. A thick padding worn on the outside of the uniform to protect the chest from foul balls. Its purpose is much like the breastplate of righteousness, which protects our hearts from the influence of our old sin nature. As new creatures in Christ, we take up the righteousness of Jesus Christ and lay aside our old ways.

3. Baseball Glove. A padded, leather hand covering used in baseball for catching thrown or batted balls. Without a glove, the catcher would have no way to defend himself against pitches hurled in his direction. The shield of faith is our protection against the fiery darts of the Enemy, such as discouragement, despair, and depression.

4. Catcher's Mask. Also called a *birdcage*, this is a protective face covering worn by a catcher or home plate umpire. It is made with strong wires that run horizontally and vertically. Our minds are a battlefield for Satan. He attacks with ruthless cunning. The helmet of salvation keeps our heads in the game and our thoughts on the Lord.

5. Cleats. These are the projecting pieces of plastic, rubber, or metal at the bottom of athletic shoes to improve traction. The Bible commands us to have our feet fitted with the readiness that comes from the gospel of peace. Bitterness and an unforgiving heart hold us back; they prevent spiritual growth and, ultimately, lead to our downfall. It's hard to get anywhere when your feet are forever slipping on the pebbles of provocation.

6. Rule Book. This is a published book containing the official rules of baseball. I'm sure there are many dog-eared copies of this in locker rooms around the nation. Millions have referred to it in the middle of a clutch situation. The Bible is a book that contains much more than rules. It is also referred to as the Sword

of the Spirit, as it can cut through any argument or problem. It is immovable, unchangeable, and invincible—the final Word.

7. Catcher's Sign. This is the means by which a catcher speaks with the pitcher. It is a display of fingers or a hand signal by the catcher to the pitcher. Without the use of the catcher's sign, the level of communication between these two crucial players would be greatly hindered. Paul exhorts the Ephesians to "pray on all occasions" (Ephesians 6:18). Communication with the Father is vital to relationship and the outcome of the game. He, like the pitcher, sees our world from a completely different angle than we do. Not only does He see the bigger picture, He knows how the game will end!

All right, girlfriends, huddle up! Our Adversary would like nothing better than to defeat us in our role as mothers. He wants us to forget about him and get overconfident in our own abilities. Unlike our Lord, he keeps close stats on all our failings. But remember, slumps come and go, and we're due for a victory! I encourage you to "be strong in the Lord and in his mighty power." Remember to accessorize in the morning with the full armor of God. Okay, now go get 'em, slugger!

WHERE CAN I GET A FAST PASS THROUGH THE TEEN YEARS?

Few things are more satisfying than seeing your own children have teenagers of their own.

DOUG LARSON

Never lend your car to anyone to whom you have given birth.

ERMA BOMBECK

I was a good teenager—at least I think I was. My mother and I had the usual power struggles. I think the most rebellious thing I ever did was to flip her off behind her back in a moment of pure pubescent weakness. Fear not: I ran downstairs to my room straightaway to beg God's forgiveness lest He smite me on the spot and send me straight to hell. I don't think I even did it right. I had to hold the other three fingers down. It didn't have the effect I'd intended. All in all, it was an anti-climactic moment of defiance.

The teen years are tough, and teens are constantly being reminded of this by all who are light-years from the teen scene. (Side note: You know you're light-years from the teen scene when you use phrases

like "teen scene.") Things are different these days, I will admit. I was an eighties kid. The biggest stress in my life was making sure my bangs were tall enough and my outfit color-coordinated, down to the last earring. Today there are no bangs to be found, and clothes (not outfits) are less a fashion statement and more a vehicle to reveal one's latest tattoo or piercing (at least that's what I hear—my kids are still preteens, so I haven't had to deal with these issues yet). In my day, nobody was pierced anywhere but their earlobes, and only retired Marines sported tattoos. I know—I'm light-years from the teen scene.

The unique pressures to fit in while not conforming to the latest social evil can be daunting for our younger generation. In addition to peer pressure, adolescence is steeped in self-doubt, insecurity, and the never-ending worries about what everyone else is thinking about "me." That's the tough part: worrying about how others view us. Wait a minute—that never changes, does it? We all struggle with self-doubt and insecurities. At least as adults, we can have some kind of perspective and maturity (or if nothing else, a well-stocked pantry full of our favorite comfort foods).

At what point in our lives do we transform from blissfully unaware children to uncertain teens? Specifically when and how does this happen? I think for most of us, the seventh grade looms as the pinnacle of our angst. The further we get from our junior high years, the easier it is to forget our insecurity prime. Those were the days when we knew the full impact of true, raw insecurity because we were confronted with it every day in the mirror.

When I was in the seventh grade, I weighed a whopping seventy pounds and could stretch to an impressive four foot six. I remember this because there was a boy who was so amused by my size that he would holler down the hallway whenever he saw me coming,

"Hey, it's Four Foot Six!" Honestly, if today's vehicle laws had been enacted two decades earlier, I would have had to bear the social strain of having to sit in a child car seat until high school. I look at my three petite children and think to myself, *Eat, for gosh sakes. Don't you realize what a booster seat will do to your sense of self-esteem as a teenager?*

In the fall of my seventh-grade year, not only was I trapped in the body of a ten-year-old but I also had metal braces and a newly permed hairdo complete with the universal big bangs. To top it off, I was excruciatingly shy. I still meet up with former classmates who ask me where I went to junior high. Sheesh.

I had a friend, though, who appeared to have missed out on the geek gland. (Don't say *geek* around your kids unless you want to see a serious rolling of the eyes.) Her name was Shannon Heaverly. Even her name is cool. My name, on the other hand, was Jenny Egge (rhymes with leggy, unfortunately). Shannon was tall, slender, and shapely, and she had naturally feathered hair. I came up to her shoulder when I was on my tiptoes.

I can still remember the first week of junior high. Shannon and I were hanging out in the vicinity of our first classroom before school started. Being your typical firstborn child, I was nervous about being late for class, so I kept my wandering to a minimum.

What I remember about girls in junior high is that they spend a lot of time talking to one another in loud voices when they are trying to get the attention of any cute boys in the area. There happened to be quite a few cute boys that day, so we were laughing and talking quite freely. Shannon tended to draw the eyes of the boys, so we were definitely the center of attention in the hall.

At one point in our conversation, Shannon said something

hilarious, and I roared with laughter. Unfortunately, at the same time, Shannon lifted her hand and tossed that feathered hair over her shoulder, and my mouth full of braces met up with her pretty baby blue sweater, smack dab in the middle of her arm.

So there I was, hooked like a salmon with a pathetic deer-in-the-headlights expression—hardly the look any junior-higher would want to show in public, let alone in front of cute boys! Shannon was unaware of my plight and for some reason imagined I was biting her on the shoulder—in front of cute boys! So she did the natural thing and started smacking me on the head in the attempt to get me away from her. In order to try to free up my trapped teeth, I had to let go of my books and notebooks, which went flying in all directions. This only aggravated Shannon's assault. I kept trying to explain the situation, but all that came out was a muffled, "Thannnnneon, I'm thuhaick on oar thwetherer!"

In a last-ditch effort to free myself from Shannon's attack, I ripped my mouth from her sweater and finally broke free. Poor Shannon leveled a look of contempt my way and stalked off without giving me a chance to explain. The bell rang, and I was left alone in the hallway amidst sprawled books with a large piece of baby blue thread hanging from my upper teeth. This was probably the most embarrassing moment of my life, but I remember thinking to myself, *Someday, someday I am going to think this story is absolutely hysterical.* It took a couple of decades, but I was right.

WHAT'S SO SCARY?

When you are a teenager, it seems that everything is just so embarrassing. One summer afternoon, my mom took me, my

younger sisters, and a few of our girlfriends clothes shopping at the local mall. You can imagine the stress of bringing an entire gaggle (as in geese) of teenage girls to the mall on a tight budget. After being dragged around the shopping mall for an entire day and shelling out the big bucks for the latest fashions, I'm sure she expected at least a little bit of appreciation. And we truly were grateful. However, as we got into the car and turned to her, we were sidetracked by a chewed piece of gum we noticed dangling from her, um, chest. She had lost her gum in the car and had sent us all searching for it hours earlier.

Unfortunately, none of us had been successful in finding it anywhere on the floor or in the seat of the car. When we all collectively realized that she had been sporting a piece of chewed Dentyne in plain view on her, um, chest all day, in front of cute boys at the mall, we completely panicked! All of her noble acts from the entire day were totally wiped clean by a piece of gum.

We're all grown up now and have children of our own. Every once in awhile, we all get away together to go on a shopping spree. There have been moments before we get out of the car when we all look to Mom and say, "Will you please check your, um, chest first?"

My dad was the only male in the household. There were three of us girls, our mother, our two female cats, and our female dog. Poor guy. And he had been an only child, so it was tough duty for a few years. He was a force to be reckoned with whenever boys came around. My dates would come to the front door, and Dad would introduce himself and proceed with the inquisition. He should have considered a second career as an FBI interrogator. Once a date passed the inspection, Dad made sure to restate the curfew (10:00 p.m., for goodness sake) a couple of times. He was a Vietnam vet who would not tolerate anyone messing with his girls. As much as

I cringed at the time, I have to thank my dad for scaring off a few undesirables.

My mom was in on the act as well. Anytime she needed to remind the boyfriend in question that he was late heading home, she would simply holler down the heat vent repeatedly until he left. She would also recruit my sisters for the show. They were happy to join in on the espionage performance. In fact, I recall they witnessed my first kiss. Embarrassing then, but funny to think about now.

What is not so funny to me is the potential reality of my future teenagers flipping me off behind my back in a moment of pubescent weakness! Good grief: dates, first kisses, dances, movies, boyfriends, girlfriends, driving—eeeek! All of a sudden, the toddler years of diapers and temper tantrums seem tame in comparison to what looms ahead on the parental horizon.

A recent trip to Disney World provided me with an inspiration for dealing with the troubling teen years: the Fast Pass. A few years ago, overcrowded theme parks came up with the idea of placeholders for the most popular attractions. You simply pick up a ticket with a time frame printed out on it. While waiting for your turn, you are free to roam, shop, and enjoy other parts of the park. Fast Passes are wonderful! We took full advantage of these delightful tickets and raced from one ride to another. The only question I had was why so many poor souls opted to wait in line for an hour and a half instead of utilizing the Fast Pass. *What a bunch of schmoes!* I would think to myself as we ran down the Fast Pass ramp right onto the ride.

For those of us worrying about and somewhat dreading our kids' teenage years, the Fast Pass idea sounds like the perfect solution. Rather than suffering through the sass-back years, I could simply take a ticket and come back when they were ready to treat

me like the Proverbs 31 woman ("Her children arise and call her blessed," verse 28).

Okay, I know that's not going to happen. A truly committed mom sticks it out with her kids, driving permits notwithstanding. I have a good friend named Debbi who has two sons in their twenties. She is the consummately good mother, always watching out for their best interests and making sure their world is in order. Translation: She is a self-proclaimed control freak! (She and I have a lot in common.) At some point between baby bottles and graduation, we mothers are supposed to figure out how to set our children free. We are to send them out on their own to make their own decisions, even if they are not the decisions we would make. I know, it makes me tremble just thinking about it. My sweet friend definitely has some experience on me, though, and has learned a thing or two in her years of parenting teenagers. A few years ago, she shared the following story at our church women's retreat:

Last summer my sixteen-year-old son, Jake, was getting ready for summer camp. He was going to be gone for a full week, and being the control-freak mom I am, I really wanted to be on top of the packing thing. After fielding a barrage of questions and reminders from me, Jake firmly asserted that he could pack for himself. I was crushed! What if he forgot his underwear or, worse, his toothbrush? I did not have a cheerful heart as I slowly walked away thinking to myself, *Doesn't he understand that I'm the mom? I need to help him. It's my job!*

The next morning, I walked downstairs and discovered his suitcase wide open on the floor. The desire to go

through it and check to see that he had everything he needed was more than my mommy-fingers could handle. However, I realized I couldn't go pawing through his stuff after his explicit words to me.

As I gawked at his packing job, I couldn't get past the first item I noticed laying on the top: lime green wool ski socks! What was he thinking? He was going to a place that would be at least ninety-five degrees! Didn't he know that the kids at camp would surely make fun of him for wearing such things? He was destined to be the outcast; certainly no one would hang with a kid who would wear such bizarre accessories. I thought to myself, *I need to protect him!* The temptation to remove the socks without telling Jake was unbelievably powerful. Well, the lime socks prevailed and I did finally walk away. It was one of the hardest mom-things I've ever had to do (I told you I'm a control freak).

A couple of hours later, we arrived at the church to meet up with his friends. We got out of the car, and Jake took his stuff out of the trunk. He kissed me good-bye and ran over to a group of teenagers. (Don't you love a sixteen-year-old boy who still kisses his mommy good-bye?) The kids hugged and high-fived him. As I slowly walked back to the car, out of the blue (or from heaven) I heard a voice say, "Hey, Jake, did you bring your lime green socks?"

I instantly stopped in my tracks, looked up with tears in my eyes, and thanked the Lord for the blessing. I realized right then and there that if I'd taken control and removed the ski socks, I would have missed the blessing,

and, more important, I would have betrayed Jake. It was a moment of clarity. While I never did find out why they needed the lime green socks—no doubt for some silly camp fun—right then I knew I'd have to start letting go of Jake. It was time to loosen the controls and allow him to take the reins himself.

an example of holiness

You know, I don't believe Debbi's story is completely unique. Oh, the lime green wool ski socks are, but the fact that God deeply loves our young people and uses them to teach *us* lessons isn't particularly unusual. In fact, God used teenagers in the Bible to perform some amazing things—seriously. Hang with me here as we learn a little from "Dan the almost-man."

Daniel was a young Hebrew, one of the sons of Israel, "young men without any physical defect, handsome, showing aptitude for every kind of learning, well informed, quick to understand, and qualified to serve in the king's palace" (Daniel 1:4). Woo-hoo, he was my kind of guy: godly, good-looking, and genuinely good. Unfortunately for Daniel's social life, he was taken prisoner at the age of fifteen by Nebuchadnezzar, king of Babylon, along with a bunch of other young bucks.

The king placed these boys in a position of honor in his royal service. They were to train and study for three years before entering into a commitment to the king. As part of their preparation, Nebuchadnezzar lavished upon these young men every luxury he could afford, including choice food and wine from his royal supply.

However, being a Jew, Daniel chose to abstain from eating the

king's meat and wine. No comfort food for this kid. The Babylonians were an ungodly lot. Their culture was steeped in idolatry and pagan traditions. The ceremonies involved with their food preparation included ritualistic sacrifice and consecration of the food to their idols of choice—something that would have been detestable to Daniel and his Israelite friends.

Scripture tells us that God had made the steward who was in charge of Daniel and his friends favorable toward Daniel. As a result of his convictions, Daniel approached the steward and requested a diet of vegetables and water for himself and his three buddies. The steward was apprehensive about the whole arrangement because he was responsible to ensure that the king's boys would someday be mighty men, and this included feeding them properly. Besides, the king's reputation was hardly one of compassion and consideration; Nebuchadnezzar was a "My way or the highway" kind of monarch. Daniel persisted. Being a guy, he sized up the situation and (of course) turned it into a competition.

> Please test your servants for ten days: Give us nothing but vegetables to eat and water to drink. Then compare our appearance with that of the young men who eat the royal food, and treat your servants in accordance with what you see. (Daniel 1:12-13)

I'm sure you can picture it: *Animal House* versus *Chariots of Fire*. After ten days, Daniel and his friends were much stronger, healthier, and more lucid than the king's good old boys. In light of Daniel's obedience, God blessed him even beyond having the steward's sympathy.

To these four young men God gave knowledge and
understanding of all kinds of literature and learning. And
Daniel could understand visions and dreams of all kinds.
(Daniel 1:17)

What's the lesson here? (I hope you don't think this is an illustration on dieting—surely you must trust me by now!) The lesson
is that God used the teenaged Daniel to set an example of holiness
in front of a completely pagan king and nation—and his mother
was nowhere near! On the other hand, God was near. He saw and
rewarded Daniel's obedience. As time passed, Daniel earned the
respect and honor of the king. In order for all of this to happen, his
mother had to be willing to let Daniel go.

Since taking this brief glimpse into Daniel's story, I am truly
convinced that if God can use a kidnapped teenager to make a
difference in history, then maybe He can use my future dear dar-
ling teenagers as well. In fact, He's probably got the whole thing all
figured out without my help at all!

So, for those future days when my children are all alone in the
world without their mother, I hereby relinquish any lingering Fast
Pass fantasies. Instead, I commit to ponder the life of Daniel and
pray for my kids instead of worrying about them. Starting now, I'll
begin the process of turning them over to God—letting them go
because I know they're in good hands. I may still invest in a miniature rearview mirror for my glasses, just in case! With God's help, I
can look to the future not with trepidation but with triumph, trusting in His plan.

more or Less

Education is a progressive discovery of our own ignorance.
WILL DURANT

I may have mentioned this before: I'm a list person. It comes with the territory of being a type A, overachieving oldest child. During the writing process of this book, I've compiled two lists. The first list is titled "The More List." These are things I have experienced *more* of since becoming a mom. The second is "The Less List"—what I have experienced *less* of since becoming a mom.

The More List. Not surprisingly, this list is composed of items such as: stretch marks, Fruit Roll-Ups, bathtub toys, child car seats, sippy cups, winter coats, and Popsicle stick collections. Moms and dads also get to experience more bubble gum, more giggling, more tickling, more ice cream, more bubble baths, more snow sledding and snowman making, more Dr. Seuss, more pancakes and cereal for dinner, and more pride—the good kind of pride, such as what you feel when your child performs in her first school play, dressed like a pink firefly. And more recycling bins! Prior to the elementary

years, I hadn't realized the volume of paperwork that daily walked in the door with each grade-schooler. Of course, the disposal of said schoolwork must be done delicately. Any and all kid-creations must be openly appreciated to the fullest extent before secretly being chucked in the big blue bin in the garage. However, every once in awhile, they go a' digging and come in the house grasping their latest spelling test with a look of utter disbelief: "Mom, how did *this* get in the recycle bin?"

I have become the expert question dodger in such situations. "Oh my. It's a good thing you found it. You better put it in your room in a safe place." (Pretty good, huh?)

The Less List. Well, this list is fairly lengthy and somewhat predictable: less sleep, free time, stomach muscle tone, uninterrupted adult conversation, and room in the hall closet for frivolous things like snow skis and tennis rackets (see "winter coats" on The More List). Less mindless television, less stagnancy, less boredom, and less selfishness. Oh, the freshness of childhood! The positive side of the lists so outweighs the negative. But we can't leave our contemplations in the playground of parenthood. As with most of our motherhood observations, the lessons we encounter can be applied beyond the backyard fence to the big picture of our lives.

This holds true for spiritual matters as well. The more we come to know the God of all creation, the less we are impressed with ourselves and the more we are humbled to see how very big He is. The beauty is that as He gets bigger in our mind, He also gets closer. In Acts 17:26-27, Luke, inspired by the Holy Spirit, wrote,

> From one man he made every nation of men, that they
> should inhabit the whole earth; and he determined

the times set for them and the exact places where they should live. God did this so that men would seek him and perhaps reach out for him and find him, though he is not far from each one of us.

God does not operate with the same limitations as man. He is above and beyond everything we could imagine. As His children, we are given the privilege of knowing Him. Isaiah 55:6 says,

> Seek the LORD while he may be found;
>   call on him while he is near.

Our God is a perfect parent: He loves us unconditionally, He is infinitely patient, He is just, He is never selfish, He is never frazzled, and He's not even fazed by the possibility of contracting Mad Cow Disease. He intimately knows our weaknesses. In fact, He teaches us through them, and He longs for us to call on Him while He may be found.

Thankfully, God doesn't require any amount of intellectual savvy in order for us to know Him. We simply need to be willing. Personally, I can't comprehend parenthood without the help of God. My weaknesses so outnumber my strengths. The other night, while reflecting on some of my failures, I murmured to my husband, who was nodding off to sleep next to me, "I'm sorry I can be such a pain."

I waited for him to alleviate my worries with a reply somewhere along the lines of "Oh, honey, you're not a pain." However, he mumbled without hesitation, "Yeah, but you can be really sweet too."

Not exactly the glowing portrayal I was hankering for. God is

determined to keep me humble! Thankfully, God's strengths more than compensate for my faults. Paul, writing to the Christians in Ephesus, said,

> I pray that out of his glorious riches he may strengthen
> you with power through his Spirit in your inner being, so
> that Christ may dwell in your hearts through faith. And I
> pray that you . . . may have power . . . to grasp how wide
> and long and high and deep is the love of Christ, and
> to know this love that surpasses knowledge—that you
> may be filled to the measure of all the fullness of God.
> (Ephesians 3:16-19)

We sure don't know everything there is to know about God. He is wider, longer, higher, and deeper than the depths of our comprehension. Yet He promises to fill us to the measure of all the fullness of Himself. And the more I focus on Him, the less I have to worry about me. Sounds like a good deal, doesn't it?

Last-mINUte mom musINɕs

We started this journey together in an attempt to explore what it means to become Real in the trenches of motherhood. We've looked at what it means to be worn-out but well loved. We've meandered through several stages of childhood, pausing to reflect on the pains and the joys, the laughter and the tears on the way to becoming a Real Velveteen Mommy. We've laughed at the ridiculously unlaughable. Daily existence is surmountable when we can chuckle about the chaos around us.

And we've vented a little about mom frustrations between the giggles. Somehow it's easier to accept the aggravations when we see the same ones reflected in the eyes of another. We've also tried to identify and claim for ourselves some of the lessons God has for us on this treacherous path of parenthood. I hope these mom musings have given you a deeper appreciation of your day-to-day parenting experiences—all of which are part of your path to becoming Real.

And I trust, dear friend, that I have communicated how gently and generously God works in my life despite the fact that I am a patience-impaired, synapse-damaged, sleep-deprived, walking and talking human plunger. My gift to you is a sampling of the few lessons gleaned through some of my everyday moments of motherhood. I pray they have made an impact on your life. More important, my wish is that you too will experience the whisperings of God in the circumstances that weave throughout your own life, because that, fellow mom, is more or less the point.

Let's conclude our journey with an exhortation in honor of the One who is the Source of all joy, hope, peace, patience, creativity, comfort, endurance, and (praise the Lord!) humor.

May the God of hope fill you with all joy and peace as you trust in him, so that you may overflow with hope by the power of the Holy Spirit. (Romans 15:13)

more or less

BY Jenn Doucette

God, the more that I know you, the less I know of you
the more I trust you, the less I fear
the more I can see you, the less I see of me
    'cause you are the one who is greater than me
the more I serve you, the less I feel worthy
the more I praise you, the less I cry
the more I love you, the less I feel hopeless
    'cause you are the one who died for me
    you are the one who is greater than me
    you are the one who died for me
the more you fill me, the less I am empty
the more I am learning, the less I know all
the more I crave Jesus, the less I seek elsewhere
    'cause you are the one who created me
    yes, you are the one who is greater than me
    oh, you are the one who died for me

notes

1. Margery Williams Bianco, *The Velveteen Rabbit* (New York: Simon & Schuster, 1989), 1.

2. Bianco, 4.

3. Bianco, 5, 8.

4. Harry Oxorn, *Human Labor and Birth*, 5th ed. (New York: McGraw-Hill, 1986), http://www.childbirth.org/articles/defepis .html.

5. Michael Card, *Come to the Cradle* (Nashville: Sparrow Press, 1993), 6.

6. http://dictionary.reference.com/search?q=kerfuffle.

7. Everett Harrison and Charles F. Pfeiffer, eds., *The Wycliffe Bible Commentary* (Chicago: Moody, 1980), 1047.

8. http://www.bartleby.com/66/73/1873.html.

9. David B. Guralnik, ed., *Webster's New World Dictionary of the American Language* (New York: Warner Books, 1987).

10. Dr. Michael Fishbane, MyJewishLearning.com.

11. http://my.homewithgod.com/heavenlymidis/kids_good.html.

12. Brother Lawrence, *The Practice of the Presence of God* (New York: Oneworld Publications, 1999), front flap.

13. Ray Vander Laan, "That the World May Know, Follow the Rabbi Faith Lessons with Ray Vander Laan," November 4, 2003, http://community.gospelcom.net/Brix?pageID=1657.

14. American Sheep Industry Association, www.sheepusa.org, http://www.sheepusa.org/index.phtml?page=site/text&nav_id =06b30b9c925056e3635d644c8ae9a29b.

15. http://www.dict.org/bin/Dict?Form=Dict2&Database=wn&Q uery='referred+pain'.

16. George MacDonald, as quoted in C. S. Lewis, *The Problem of Pain* (Glasgow, Great Britain: William Collins Sons, 1940), vi.

17. Willy Welch, copyright 1986. Playing Right Music, 9048 Mercer Place, Dallas, TX 75228.

18. *Enlexica Baseball Dictionary*, May 4, 2004, http://www .enlexica.com/sp/bb/.

about the author

JENN DOUCETTE is the mother and caregiver of three children, eight chickens, and a cat (and one beta fish, who doesn't look like he'll make it through the week). As an author and speaker, Jenn loves to hold up the half-empty glass of motherhood, flavor it with juice from the lemons of life, and stir it all together with the sweetness of humor.

In 1992, Jenn married Ben Doucette and earned a bachelor of arts degree in psychology (an irony not lost on her). She has coauthored a devotional book for teens with Tim Baker titled *Live It Real* (Fleming/Revell, 2006) and is currently working on her next mommy book. Jenn, Ben, and company make their home in Snohomish, Washington.

You can contact Jenn either through e-mail (benjenn@bigfoot .com) or by checking out her website (http://www.daisyministries .com).

MORE RESOURCES FOR MOMS.

Habits of a Child's Heart

Gain the tools and specific ideas you need to intentionally develop your child's faith. Learn about spiritual disciplines such as study, meditation, service, and worship for yourself—then teach them to your kids.

Valerie E. Hess and Marti Watson Garlett   1-57683-427-1

Talkers, Watchers, and Doers

Create a tailor-made learning environment for each of your children, equipping them with specialized study skills to match their unique personalities.

Cheri Fuller   1-57683-599-5

Raising Motivated Kids

Packed with dozens of helpful hints, this book will show you how to turn your parental insight into powerful motivation to help your kids succeed in life.

Cheri Fuller   1-57683-601-0

School Starts at Home

Discover how you can foster a stimulating, creative environment for your children by modeling a love of learning at home.

Cheri Fuller   1-57683-600-2

Visit your local Christian bookstore,
call NavPress at 1-800-366-7788, or log on to www.navpress.com
to purchase.

To locate a Christian bookstore near you,
call 1-800-991-7747.

NAVPRESS
BRINGING TRUTH TO LIFE
www.navpress.com